THE TANGLED PATH TO GLORY

A Novel Approach to One
Man's Search for the Infinite Connection

RUSSELL S. OYER

Order this book online at www.trafford.com
or email orders@trafford.com

Most Trafford titles are also available at major online book retailers.

Printed in the United States of America.

ISBN: 978-1-4669-5853-1(sc)
ISBN: 978-1-4669-5852-4(e)

Trafford rev. 09/18/2012

 www.trafford.com

North America & International
toll-free: 1 888 232 4444 (USA & Canada)
phone: 250 383 6864 ♦ fax: 812 355 4082

for

NANCY, TIM, and SARA,
WHO HAVE MADE IT ALL SEEM WORTHWHILE

ACKNOWLEDGEMENTS

Thanks go to both Dr. Robert F. Jackson and Dr. Dave Roe for encouraging me and thoughtfully offering help while cheering me to continue with this project. And to Dr. Kathy Gribbin who helped along the way. Thank you to my nephew, Dave Oyer, whose interest, enthusiasm, and suggestions were of great value. Also to my brother-in-law and dear friend, Gary Habegger, who digitized my old typewritten pages. My gratitude to my son-in-law, Lee Hall, for the cover photo. And finally, thanks to my daughter, Sara Oyer Hall, who proofread, edited, encouraged, and without whose help this project would not have been completed.

Contents

I

The Mystery

"For now we see through a glass darkly." Saint Paul

There is no pleasure, no mystery, no problem of our physical world that does not point to a mystery beyond itself. All avenues taken by our physical, mental or spiritual searchings ultimately lead to an insoluble, infinite problem. The farther we extend our searching, the more we realize we are enslaved by the very thing we seek: that is, our inability to extricate ourselves from the problem. For the same compounds that are causing the sun to burn on endlessly are also a part of our earth and makeup, even our brain itself.

As the physicist Niels Bohr once stated, "We are both spectators and actors in the great drama of existence." Shakespeare points at the same problems. "Life is but a walking shadow, a poor player that struts and frets his hour upon the stage and then is heard no more. It is a tale, told by an idiot, full of sound and fury, signifying nothing." (MacBeth 5:5)

Lincoln Barnett in his book, *The World and Dr. Einstein*, makes the following statement. "Man's inescapable impasse is that. He himself is part of the world he seeks to explore; his body and proud brain are mosaics of the same elemental particles that compose the dark drifting dust clouds of interstellar space; he is, in the final analysis, merely a conformation of the space-time field, standing midway between macrocosm and microcosm, he finds barriers on every side."

It has always seemed to me to be incongruous of God to have so important a thing as existence thrust upon me without so much as a, "Do you mind?" or "Would you like to?" asked of me. I have thought much about this question and have come to the conclusion that certainly God has something really astonishing for each one of us to do that would make our becoming important enough for Him to bypass this rather simple courtesy.

It is to this conclusion that in the next few pages, I, like Virgil, would like to lead the reader. I have used times and places from my own life and have purposely treated them at times humorously and at other times seriously. In using my own life, I hope to strike a responsive chord like "I've felt like that too" from the reader. In doing this, I also hope that in some small way to have acted as a spiritual midwife in your re-birth as you too must find the path to Glory, though tangled it might be.

II

Beginnings

He hammered, He wrought me . . . So purely,
So palely, tinily, surely, mightily, frailly.
Francis Thompson

I was an untamed sort upon whom the usual methods of discipline had very little effect. I was a person of indomitable will and abundant energy. A person who monopolizes every conversation, organizes every game, leads the charge, and in general does the things of life very well. This fact, one supposes, is the reason for other members of the group letting a person of this temperament take over. Mainly, he gets the job done.

Be not mistaken: thoughtfulness, care, love or benefit of the group is not the motivation for doing the job. One feels first and foremost the thrill of the organization, the thrill of seeing your plans in action, the thrill of bending people to your will, the thrill of reveling in pure action, motion, movement, is accomplishment, if you will. This was the motivation I felt. I was, and still am, in fact, a genius at organization.

A person (unfortunately, because it can be a great curse) that accomplishes vast amounts of work simply by organizing it so efficiently sometimes causes others to think you are loafing until suddenly the job is done.

Here in lies a very frustrating part of my temperament. I cannot find a job that contains enough challenging work to keep me busy. Thus, boredom and consequently daydreaming about other challenging thoughts tend to creep into my mind. When this happens, one has a tendency to form bad mental and physical habits. I tend to lapse into lethargy, apathy, and finally depression. I also tend to be very goal oriented and utilitarian. If I see no goal or use out there, then simply I will not work on the problem. Do not be deluded into believing that the goal or use has to be tangible or materialistic. There again is a frustration of this temperament. As one strives for the glory or the praise that should come, it generally trickles in because of most peoples' ignorance of the problem and their lack of realization of just what is involved in its solution.

My brother had the slow moving disposition of our father. Because of this, he bent easily to my will. I can only remember fighting with him once. This started as a friendly wrestling match that eventually got out of hand. He was content to live in my shadow and be a bright spot in my aura.

I can remember running about with his friends. I have some great remembrances of wild evenings with that group as they were testing their wings. They were literally "Hell on Wheels," the wildest bunch of drivers I have even to this day seen!

Floods of memories at this point sweep over my intellect. In fact, my heart is pounding with fear right now and my knuckles are white against this desk as I think of those hair-raising rides around Belaire. The night crossing the 28 rail crossing of the Nickel Plate in a '46 Mercury with 14 kids in the car without the benefit of the regular street crossing. Our internal organs were never the same to say nothing of the shocks on the car. Or driving across the Sheridan Park Golf Course at midnight with the authorities in chase, slowing down only to pull the pins from the greens—talk about playing through. Missing the turn at the end of Fulton Street and plunging over the edge into the river and driving a mile, along the river bed till we found a place to emerge up the bank to the road again. I am perplexed at this point as just what to include as literally hundreds of these vignettes have fluttered through my mind bringing with them the fear and physical uncomfort that belongs to facing instant death.

There is, of course, one great story that stands head and shoulders above all the rest. My brother and I were cast by the fates in starring roles. To skip this story would certainly make me remiss in telling the events leading to my discovery of the ultimate thrill or joy of living.

There was a youngster who lived next door to us whom we shall call Joey. Joey was an emaciated kid, fully the runt of the litter and a poor result of malnutrition. Joey was the kid we would beat up and pummel just for practice or to keep in shape. There is always one kid in every peer group who keeps asking for it. Joey was that kid, and we obliged him by giving it to him.

It so happened that God had smiled upon my brother and me to give us the gifts of being rather handy with tools. We also had the materials to build. We had in those days a fascinating pastime which we termed trash-can-hunting. Pure and simple, this was merely looking through the hardware throwaways of the local tradesmen. Some highly prized articles were wheels and tin or pipe of any kind.

On one of these soirees, we had the good fortune of finding four large scooter wheels and about fifteen square feet of galvanized steel. We were delirious with ecstasy. Our fondest dreams were now coming to fruition as we sat down to plan our "crator".

The untutored might ask at this point for a definition of a crator. Loosely defined, a crator is a desecrated form of the famous soap box derby cars without the rules governing its plan, size, weight or use. The crator was about five feet long and about three feet wide consisting of 4x4s and 2x4's. The seat was a bucket seat from a '34 Chevy. The hood was then totally encased in galvanized steel and nailed to the frame with twenty penny spikes. Across the front, we put a 2x12 (native) four foot long board and onto this we affixed two 3/4" pipes four feet long. We, for a time, had fixed the metal part of a pitchfork onto the front, however our father quickly put an end to this "nonsense" as he preferred to call it.

To understand clearly what is involved, one must visualize the physical aspects of the local geography (see the figure below).

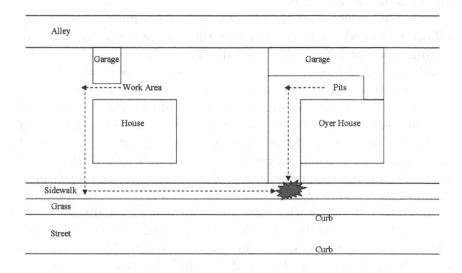

Our crator was the envy of the neighborhood mainly because of its durability. The bliss or joy of the whole escapade was the ramming or annihilation of others, their persons and property without so much as a scratch on you or your crator. This was relatively easy for us to do as our crator was approximately 260 pounds, far outweighing those of the rest of the neighborhood.

Joey wanted a crator, too, so his father journeyed down to the local grocer and picked up an orange crate that had just made the lazy, comfortable trip from sunny Florida. To this scant orange crate of 1/8" slats he affixed four buggy wheels (spoked type) from his sister's play baby carriage. This little drama took several days. My brother and I noted all this hustle and bustle from the pit area in our backyard. Joey's father had painted this wobbly contraption, a light baby blue enamel. The paint was just dry, and they were putting the finishing touches on their crator while Jim, another neighbor, helped. We watched ominously from our pit area.

At last!!!!!! The great day had come! Joey, his father and neighbor Jim were going through last minute instructions like a launch countdown. Those last words of Joey's dad will always ring in my ears as long as this diaphram will continue to function. I quote, "Joey, you had better be careful of the Oyer boys!"

I heard my brother chuckle nervously as he too heard those words, and I felt the thrill and joy of the hunt. My heart began to pump faster in anticipation of the inevitable.

Now keep one eye here and one eye back at the geographical layout as the story unfolds.

From his backyard with Joey driving and Jim pushing, they were off on their maiden voyage. The only thing missing was the bottle of champagne, but I doubt if the small craft could have withstood the bombardment. Most certainly the crator would have been broken and not the bottle. As they went north to the side of their house, Joey's dad was ecstatic (somewhat like I would assume the father of Columbus) as he watched with longing in his eyes as his son went off to conquer new worlds. It was certainly a touching sight. The frail craft then turned west along the north side of Joey's house finally to the sidewalk. Ah, the moment of decision. Here, like all great decisions, (Hitler's invasion of Poland, the atomic bomb on Heroshima, my going to Indiana or Purdue), the fates hung on every thought, on every word spoken, waiting for a definite go that would shape lives, change destinies, leave the direction of this earth to hang motionless until it is made. If . . . ah, there lies the rub, if the stuff dreams are made of . . . if the pale craft would have turned north, perhaps our lives would have all been different. Perhaps, Ford would have never made the Edsel, but, alas, as fate would determine, some quirk of the gods jerked the wheels south (probably a stone in the grass).

We could hardly believe our ears. The beautiful sound of those wheels coming along the sidewalk south, not north. Oh, the joy, the thrill of it all! We readied ourselves for the challenge ahead. Much like that of the gladiator entering the arena, or the Buana as he faces the charge of the bull-elephant with an empty gun and loads of nerve.

We pushed out of the pits silently, our hearts pounding so loud we were afraid we both would hear the other and know that the thrill of the kill was terribly exciting. My brother was driving and I was pushing. We heard the sound coming closer of that poor little module crammed with the soon to be remains of the human life.

The veins on my neck and arms stood out and my heart was at the bursting point as I gave complete and total effort. We picked up speed rapidly, faster, faster, faster. Now the small blue object was in sight. We could see the look of terror in the eyes of both driver and pusher. As our driveway sloped toward the street, more speed came easily. The blue module was now directly on the sidewalk in front of the driveway, and we were almost on it at blinding speed.

Then, a blood curdling yell, splitting of wood and the flying of wheels, parts and bodies. And just as suddenly it was all over; the quiet was deafening. What was left of Joey was lying in a huddled mass against the curb on the opposite side of the street. Joey's dad was standing at the corner of his house with an unbelievable look in his eyes. He stood stoically for a time unable to comprehend the sight before his eyes.

Meanwhile, my brother walked calmly over to the whimpering boy and said, "Are you hurt, Joey?"

This remark seemed to give Joey's dad the impetus he needed to move into action. He swept down from the slight hill, strode over to his sniveling offspring, swooped him into his arms and disappeared into the darkness of their domicile.

In the words of my father to my mother after his discovery that no one was seriously hurt and a "stern reprimand" to us, "If boys won't be boys, who will be boys?"

*　　*　　*

My father was perhaps one of the finest God-like men that has ever lived. His faith in the Living Christ was one of such completeness as he showed it in love to his family and concern for those who lived around him. His prayer life was something so alien to life today it wouldn't be believed even by most evangelical Christians currently. He was a man of immense faith and small stature, neither of which led him into abnormal thought. He was widely known for his faith and how it was the the guiding principle of his total life and that of his family.

On one of our many father-son talks, he related to me the following story that made no small impression on me.

My dad began telling the story. "I was born again (converted) at the age of six when my father was praying at family worship. My dad asked my brother if he wanted him to pray for him. My brother said yes, and then dad asked me if he should pray for me, and of course, I said yes also. Then as my father was praying, I found myself listening to what he was saying, and it dawned on my just what I was doing. Here I was giving my entire life, hopes and dreams over to this person JESUS CHRIST."

My dad continued, "I thought about this experience for many years. One day, (I must have been about eighteen), I was alone in a twenty acre corn field. It was late November and the snow was blowing quietly against my face. A team of horses was pulling the large wagon slowly along close to the rows of corn. I was walking along the row shucking the corn off each stock and shoving it into the wagon. The wind was whistling, the snow blowing and the sound of the horse's hooves echoed against the gray November sky. The only other sound was that of the cobs hitting the bottom of the wagon. In this atmosphere, the mind settles into deep thought."

"At this point, my mind began to think about what God through Christ had done for me that day back in our living room a dozen years earlier. The thought of all that was involved in my redemption overwhelmed me and completely engulfed my entire being. The JOY, the THRILL, the GREAT PURPOSE in life to know that you are guiltless, free, redeemed, was staggering."

And my dad went on, "I was so filled with joy that I think I scared the horses by my shouting and singing. This experience has made me a totally different person. It has changed my family, business and social life. I have learned not to take the situations or experiences in this life too seriously because all things, including my life, are controlled by Him who made all things. There is then, really, no permanence or stability here if your philosophy or religion or anything else, is not anchored to the eternal Christ Jesus. Therefore, everything I have and anything that I do is based upon my conversion to Jesus Christ and my communion with Him."

It was this Christian experience that my father lived and evangelized until his death in 1972.

Since I am here discussing my relationship with my father, a word about his passing might fit into the narrative at this point. Unless one has gone through the heartache of the prolonged dying of a loved one the next paragraph will make little sense.

When I used the term "loved one" I do not necessarily mean that biological coincidence of blood relatives. As the old saying goes, friends you can choose, relatives you have to accept. In fact, when my grandfather died, I felt nothing. I felt no loss. I had no memories, no regrets. For someone to be loved, I believe you must have regrets at their passing. I do not believe one can love without having regrets while looking back on your relationship together.

It was this kind of loved one that my father was. His passing deeply puzzled me and affected my life to a greater extent than most other experiences in my life except my conversion.

So it was with this background and with these relationships at home that I began the quest for the ultimate thrill or purpose for my existence.

III

The Thrill of Education

"The ill-timed truth we might have kept—
Who knows how sharp it pierced and stung?"
Edward R. Sill

Three blocks over and four blocks down sat a rather new school.
I never knew for whom it was named and didn't really care for that
matter. Many times I was embarrassed to be asked what school
I attended. When asked, I usually lowered my head and voice and
muffled my mouth as I muttered the name of my school. I would have
gladly preferred the name P.S. 28 or P.S. 114 because this had the style
of the Cagney movies or even some counterpart to the Catholic Saint
Dominic's or the like.

I should be quick to point out that the name may have been less
than P.S. 241, but the education was of the first order. I have yet to
figure out if I did well because I was an above average student, or
if I was an above average student because of the superior education
I received in those formative years. Looking back now with sixteen
years of teaching experience myself, I can see that my elementary
school teachers were some of the best I have ever encountered. They
were highly educated, excellent motivators.

Here, I found the first thrill of vicarious action in reading as I
savagely devoured book after book. I especially remember my fifth
grade instructor. Oh, the sweetness of first love! Here was the first
member of the opposite sex that spoke to my blood although she nor
I ever knew it at the time. I recall the summer of 1948 when all of us

young guys (10 years old) wanted to get her address and cruise by on our bicycles hoping to catch a glimpse of her in some daring adornment or intriguing occupation about the yard. Of course, she never was and we really didn't care because the thrill seemed to be in thinking up the plan and putting it into action. The actual fruition of the plan would seem anticlimactic to the great ideas we had imagined!

Most of us could read before we entered school, but here was the real pleasure of living, the excitment of vicarious action. I began to form a scholarly approach to literature and an appreciation for the classics with my mentor prodding me on. She had a chart that had everyone's name on it and a place where you could paste a small replica of a book beside your name for every book (of her choice) that you read and orally reported to her. She would question you regarding the content and a special test was given two weeks after the oral report. Thus, she was testing the two great properties of reading, comprehension and retention. When one had successfully passed these hurdles, you could paste the replica on the chart. She added to the chart almost daily as most of the youngsters were extending their bookshelf. We devoured the library in this small elementary school. In fact, the principal kept busy bringing books in from the downtown public library. It was here I was introduced to the paraphrases of *Beowulf, Treasure Island, Return of the Native* and hundreds of classics that have burned into my mind and have become a part of my thinking. Some might say I have missed something since I completely skipped reading *The Bobbsy Twins* and *Mystery at Chimney Rock*. Somehow, I don't think so.

I was so enthralled with the paraphrase of the *Odyssey* I wanted to start Greek then, but somehow the only Greek I've had since has been self-taught. In recent years, I have poured over the Greek New Testament with a lexicon at my fingertips.

This love of the classics led me into great wanderings in literature in high school that I never thought existed, but more about that later. At any rate, here under the tutelage of this fine teacher, I thought this was the ultimate thrill; the joy was supreme.

But, alas, this thrill though stimulating, sublime and long lasting, did not quench like water the depths of the insatiable thirst of what I have come to know as me.

I cannot say enough for the six years I spent in this institution of learning. I consider reading the ability that is the cornerstone of all learning. One might argue this point to say that experiential learning is the building block of learning. I think experience can be faulted on two counts. (Notice use of the word faulted and not discounted, because there is definitely a place for experiential learning).

1. Experience is colored by the emotions. When emotions play a part in the learning, truth seems to be relegated to a relative role. No two people explaining the same physical, mental, or spiritual experience will describe it in precisely the same manner. Emotions need to be under the strictest control or inevitably they will lead the truth of the situation down Dante's proverbial "primrose path".
2. Second, the range of experience of most of God's human beings is so dismally small that for them to draw a conclusion from their narrow field of experiential vision would be foolishness and absurdity.

Not only were the excellencies of reading taught, but also the basics of science and mathematics. People are astounded and think me inane when I tell them of the fraction, decimal, square root and verbal problems we solved easily in the third and fourth grade. The only weak area in this whole system (and I'm still feeling it today) was in art and music.

I don't, at this point, want to be too cruel in my judgment of the art and musicprogram because in my personality there is something that revolts at much of what is called art today. For example, the vision of garbage thrown at canvas and calling it art, or a few no-talent kids pounding trash can lids together and amplifying their hollerings like a wounded buffalo calling its mate. To top it off, young and old flock to them like flies over a manure pile.

Also, let me make an aside about "Christian" popular music. Some of the music we have been passing off as new "Christian" music to appeal to the youth, even in our evangelical churches, is the garbage of the youth movement wrapped in a few phrases like "loving one another", "unity", "brotherhood." All those trite phrases have nothing to do with the central truth of the Christian Faith. They have skirted the periphery of Christian thought to use words and phrases that sound Christian, but deny the cardinal doctrines of God's and man's basic natures and the problems of this life as revealed to us in Scripture.

In religious music, perhaps I am most influenced by childhood because I think the old standards of the church still have the purest melody and lyrics that say what the church is supposed to still be saying. Luther's works, the Wesley brothers, and it might seem odd to the reader, but the Christmas carols are perhaps the best of my thoughts of Christian music.

I enjoy Handel's Messiah, but become antsy until I hear the parts most familiar to me. It is, however, such a thrill or joy to rise with the chorus and full orchestra and sing, (there may be some doubt as to the use of that word sing in my case), the exciting strains of the *Hallelujah Chorus*. My heart nearly bursts and chills run up my spine as a thousand voices sing of our Savior.

> Crown Him King of Kings and Lord of Lords,
> And His name shall be called Wonderful, Counselor,
> The Mighty God, the Everlasting Father,
> The Prince of Peace.
> Amen.

IV

A Time for Loving

"Breathes there a man with soul so dead,
Whom to himself hath never said, This is my home . . ."
Sir Walter Scott

Upon leaving the tower of education each day, I would head home to another aspect of pleasure.

There was, of course, in almost every home of those days, a rather large cumbersome dark box in the living room. Emanating from that box poured forth thousands of hours of pure joy. The radio was an integral part of life around us and continued to be until its demise in the late fifties when the stations gave up working at programming and gave their airwaves over to the Top 100 hits with all that banging and clattering of pie pans and amplified guitars.

It was the radio-like books and reading which opened up large vistas of vicarious living. If it was books that gave me the love and desire for the classics and search for the truth, then radio opened my life to the love of humor. Ever since those days of sitting around the radio listening to the tales of Amos and Andy, Fibber McGee and Hubert Updike, my love for humor and the subtle joke has increased pointedly day by day. In fact, some thirty years later, my mind is astoundingly clear on many of the shows that aired in those days.

Every so often in moments of reverie, pictures of Willie and Shuffle picking up a 2x4, Pine Ridge Arkansas, the great horse Silver, Bret Reid, Lolly Baby, Captain Marvel and thousands more bring a wry

---

smile to my face. Many of my students think I am slightly (some more than slightly) dazed or, on the other hand, psychic of sorts.

Thinking of those days bring a feeling of "they were the better days" attitude to my mind. I have tried to analyze this problem to see objectively if those were really the "better days." I think in one great sense they were. Let me draw a visual picture for you.

My dad would come home from work about 4:30pm. At this time, my father, brother, and I would proceed to do any and all of the household jobs needing attention. Such jobs would include gardening (that horrible garden), mowing, outdoor sweeping, trimming, trash clean up and disposal, screens and storm windows on or off, and hundreds of other little domestic duties to help dad. Dinner would be at precisely 6:00pm and everyone was expected to BE THERE ready to ask the blessing and eat together. Dinner must be over by 6:30 because *The Lone Ranger* came on at 6:30pm every Monday, Wednesday, and Friday.

At this time, no matter what was going on or what time of year, everything came to a screeching halt. Sometimes we would listen with neighbors, sometimes the entire family. It is those times I remember most. Dad would sit in a large, over-stuffed, green chair in front of the large front window and gently unfold *The Sentinel*, always *The Sentinel*, for we were Republicans, ROCK-RIBBED REPUBLICANS. Once, when discussing politics, someone mentioned a certain person and said that he was a Democrat. A remark to which my grandmother replied, "My goodness, all these years I thought he was a Christian."

My mother would be in the kitchen doing up the dinner dishes while my brother and I were stretched out on the floor intently struggling to hear every word. To the first strains of the *William Tell Overture*, everything in the house must keep silent except the brown box with its seemingly thousands of buttons lining the front of its magnificent chest. It always seemed to me that radio was somewhat like what I could imagine the cockpit of today's moon capsule might be.

On they came like soldiers marching to Praetoria: Freeman Gosden, Charles Correll, Jack Benny, Don Wilson, Mr. D.A., Loralie Kilburn, Superman, Firefighters, Mr. First Nighter, Lux Radio Theater, Gangbuster, Mr. Keene, Boston Blackie, The Shadow, Inner Sanctum, Moon River Girl, Nick Carter, The Thin Man . . . I could go on and on. It seems now when I think of them, I see fire flickering in the fireplace, dad in the green chair reading *The Sentinel*, mom washing dishes, and my brother and I listening to every word.

Some might say how could this be so great—where was the family communication? Well, it certainly wasn't during the beloved radio time! It was during the odd job period with Dad, Saturday mornings before play, Sunday afternoons (especially as we got older), but most of all, it was during a time my father called, "Read and Pray."

Just how best to describe this time is rather difficult. True, it was a time of Bible reading and prayer where the whole family learned to pray and praise the Lord (and I don't mean whooping and hollering praising), but it was more than that. This communication time was when my parents shared what they wanted for us. We also discussed current world problems, our current youth problems, a resume of my parents and ancestor's experience, a discussion of Biblical principles for our lives, a catechism of Christian doctrine and dogma, and an exegesis of Scripture, a critical analysis of the things which we had heard over the radio and much more.

It was that time (which I fear is most lacking in family life today) when it was pure and foremost the family cloistered together around the family fires where all were safe and loved. To use a colloquialism, it was, "The family first and the rest of the world can wait."

It was also that kind of an atmosphere and attitude that no matter what problems I faced or how badly I was beaten, I always had a place of safety, of refuge for the body, mind, spirit and soul. I always felt I could retreat into the family if the way became excruciating. Many times, I longed for freedom to fly and test my wings. This freedom always had inherent in it, the nest waiting, should I dash my wings or be shot by some errant hunter. Not once did I ever entertain the notion of running away from home. I must say I had rebellious years, but never did I desire that there was any place where I was treated better than by the family onto whom I was thrust for those few years from birth to college.

V

Indian Summer

The flowers do fade, and wanton fields
To wayward winter reckoning yields . . .
Sir Walter Raleigh

Fall has always been my favorite time of year as the trees begin
to turn to gold, rust, and all the shades of brown. I revel in the beauty
of God's earth. Those are days of lingering summer warmth. There is
the beautiful "Indian Summer" that comes to Indiana about the end
of October every year. I have traveled in almost every state in the U.S.
and visited outside also, but there really is nothing to compare with a
slightly overcast day of Indian Summer in Indiana.

The light gray sky streaks down to the horizon and contrasts with
the multi-colored fall leaves. The ground is dry and the air is still,
but with just enough bite in it to say that winter is coming, yet warm
enough for a person to be in a sweater or sweatshirt. There is nothing
like walking through the woods with somebody you love on a day
like this. The brown leaves drift softly off the trees. Your feet make
crunching sounds in the dryer fallen ones. Hickory nuts and walnuts
are everywhere to be taken back for winter's use.

I always found a stick at the beginning of a walk. One always had
to have a weapon in case of a marauding bear, rattlesnake, or other
dangerous species. However, the weapon was usually used to bat
stones in the lake or strike at falling leaves. Here is the last fling at the
carefree summer life before the realities of God's purification called
winter.

I always knew at this time of year that my two favorite holidays were not far behind, Thanksgiving and Christmas. Thanksgiving was and is even this day spent with family and close friends. Always, a delicious meal was laid before us at noon. Then the afternoon was usually spent playing outside. As we got older, talk, conversation and TV football inside became the fare.

Christmas, however, was a whole other ballgame. As soon as the Thanksgiving dishes had been washed and put away, preparations were in order for Christmas. As children, we would hound my father incessantly until we made that trip out to choose the Christmas tree. This was a decision of astronomical magnitude. We searched lot after lot until we found exactly the tree that the fates had ordained would be in our home. It must always be straight, with long, full branches and a nice single top. Now that I write this, it seems ridiculous that we shopped so long and hard for only those three qualifications. In fact, I looked for those qualifications, until I finally succumbed to an artificial one a few years ago, but I still think only God can make a tree.

Anyway, with the tree now in the garage, the next step was to bug the folks until we put it up. Finally, the night came, usually about December 5th or 6th. Mother would pop a gargantuan bowl of popcorn. We thought every year we would string it on the tree, but every year the same thing always happened. In our zeal to get the tree up, we would nibble at the corn until at last it was gone before we could put it on the tree. I still think my folks planned it that way because they were not anymore eager than we were to push that needle through every kernel of corn.

It took several hours of work in the basement with a hatchet to get the tree in the base we used from year to year. Of course, all of our straightness hunting seemed to be for naught when we finally got the tree in the base. Yes, it was crooked. I think maybe the cold December weather does something to the vertical vision especially on "Honest Harry's Christmas Tree Lot." With much pomp and circumstance, the tree was brought up from the basement and placed in its honored place in the living room. Then the real work began.

The trip to the attic was a joy in itself. The attic was a virtual storehouse of goodies through which we were allowed only once a year to rummage. The Christmas things were boxed neatly, clearly labeled and placed close to the edge of the porthole to the attic. However, we always had difficulty in finding them mainly because we wanted to go through the junk in the attic. We always found toys up there we had forgotten about and had somehow mysteriously found their way to the attic since our last tenure with them.

On one occasion when we were older, (12 and16), I found the old Caterpillar tractors my brother and I had gotten for Christmas several years back. I still remember the joy I had as I once again played with these articles of years past. I don't think it was so much a feeling of love for the use of the article (as we were beyond the age of this toy), but rather, I think it was in remembering the joy I had with its play earlier in life.

So again there is that same conclusion coming back to haunt me. The joy or thrill is not in the use or possession of any tangible object, but rather in what your mind feels or thinks is the joy in seeing it out there; in the feeling or remembering it or bringing it from the dark recesses of your brain where it has been giving satisfaction for years. So the conclusion: The prize is nothing, but the striving is the actual end. The striving becomes an end in itself. Therefore, the love of the holiday and the holiday season is inherent in any happy family. I believe that one is a sign of the other, and one cannot happen without the other.

Pushing this conclusion further, I have noticed in my life and others I love, that the feeling's of love for the holiday season (Thanksgiving and Christmas in our culture) is directly proportional to the elation or depression of mind during this time of year. Recent studies prove the point that more suicides happen just after the Christmas holidays and the first week in January. I have learned as I grow older that one must strive at Christmastime to be thankful and share with one another (also to those not of your own family) or else the season becomes stale and lifeless, and we forget the elation of the season regardless of the knowledge of the real meaning of Christmas, Christ's birth.

Therefore, those that say Christmas is for children do err. Those that say Christmas is materialist do err, and those that say the proverbial "bah-humbug" do err also. The real truth (other than the obvious commemoration of Christ's birth) is that in giving of ourselves and our physical property, we do elevate our own personal mental stability. Perhaps then, with the element of real association with the living Christ, here is a beginning point of the permanent establishment of joy and purpose in one's life.

As this glorious time of year came, I began to think more deeply on these subjects and just perhaps GOD and I were closing in on one another, even a direct confrontation was in the offing.

VI

Stop Gap

Factā, Non Verbe

It should be at this point I interject the following narrative concerning the pursuit of the ultimate thrill, joy, or purpose in my life. It fits here chronologically but not necessarily in terms of the outcome of my search. I mention it only because the whole picture would be somewhat blurred, and the problems the reader faces might be somewhat akin to this one. I hesitate to mention it because the experience made very little affect on my life where it should have been the most traumatic.

February 1, 1949 our family was having "Read and Pray" time. My brother and I were rather cutting up. I remember almost word-for-word the conversation. It made an indelible impression on my mind, but did very little to my actions. My father had just said that God knew the names of every star, and I made a wise crack, smart aleck statement like, "You mean Johnny Star or Harry Star." I received a mild tongue-whipping and we went to prayer. My dad and mom then asked me if I wanted that night to receive Jesus Christ in my life. I had an overpowering feeling of dread and depression come over me like shock waves, and I was immediately sorry for the impish remarks of just a few minutes earlier and the general misbehavior of recent years. I, of course, said yes to my parent's question and the feeling of dread and depression passed. I had no visions, no violins played and not much change in my mental approach to the subject. In fact, I got more of a thrill or joy from pounding poor Joey with our crator than I had that night. To me, there is a powerful lesson here.

Whenever we let "feelings and emotions" rule our experience with God, I believe we are on dangerous ground. This is not to say that there are definitely some people, because of their emotional makeup, have an emotional high accompanying their experience with God. It is not the high emotion or low emotion that sets them into God's family. It is the fact of Jesus Christ taking over the life through his eternal sacrifice that does the job. No amount of whooping, shouting or cold rationality for that matter can accomplish this.

None-the-less, I felt not one bit different than before I prayed for forgiveness and for Christ to take over my life. In fact, I knew what the Bible said and believed it. Then I felt glad and almost as quickly thought on other things.

Now I definitely had a problem. I knew how a Christian acted. Hadn't I seen my father perform the Christian life every day? Did I not know and observe hundreds of Christians and their lives and how a Christian should act and think. There is the problem. Each day I tried to "act" like a Christian should, by what I saw in those about me. It is at this point I feel most Christians lose the battle for victorious Christian living. The problem quickly degenerated as each moment I found myself falling short of what I thought God had for my life. As I moved into adolescent years, it became difficult for me to reconcile the Christian life (as I conceived it) with the world about me.

The story is told about a rather smart, young man during the Civil War who decided not to be a part of the way. He wanted to be neutral and get along in this life with both warring factions, so he decided to wear the blue jacket of the Union and the gray pants of the Confederacy. Feeling this would accomplish his desire for neutrality, he ventured forth. Needless to say, when he was seen by either side they both shot at him. This was my feeling exactly. Instead of the thrill and the joy, I was frustrated, beaten, and defeated. The more I tried, the more I failed. The more I failed, the more I turned to other pursuits to gain the old magic, the old thrill for which I was searching.

In fact, I was worse off mentally and physically, (perhaps not spiritually), than before my conversion.

DEFEAT—APATHY—DEPRESSION

VII

Shangri-La

I should like to rise and go
Where the golden apples grow;
Where below another sky
Parrot islands anchored lie,
And watched by cockatoos and goats,
Lonely Crusoes building boats.
Robert Louis Stevenson

Every so often, something happens during our short tenure here on earth that affects the thinking, direction, and manufacture of our lives. One of these fortuitous events occurred late in 1949.

Each summer for several years, we had been going to a small lake in northern Indiana for a couple of weeks. In November of 1949, my father purchased a lake front lot on the lake with which we had become so familiar. This seemingly insignificant event led to perhaps the tightening of our family circle even more and the pleasure that only a love of nature can give.

As a family project, we began to plan to build a summer place. We rented a place on the north end of the lake for two weeks hoping that we would have our new place under roof by the end of this time. It was hard arduous work. I remember digging the foundation, water line, and septic systems by hand. I came in nights totally exhausted with blisters, then calluses over the blisters. There was no use of a power saw because the electric company had not run the lines back there in time for us to start. Everything was done by hand. This experience in itself was rapturous as I saw the labor of our hands taking shape and springing out of the ground. From this nightmarish work, I learned a very valuable and lasting lesson. This principle has helped me immeasurably time after time during my life. It has changed my attitude and thinking about work, and it is, I believe, the same pioneer spirit that made our country and won the west.

In essence, it is this. No matter the size of the job or the hardship, if one will just work at a regular pace (not breaking your neck or loafing) and hold on tenaciously, disciplining one's self to the cause or goal, bearing the inconvenience, the job will get done. One person can literally move mountains given these criteria. This sounds so simple and so easy, but I have seen literally hundreds of young people move through my classes with so little of this spirit that I don't think it exists much anymore. It is my belief that without this spirit, a nation, a race, a family, a marriage, an individual cannot survive. I think physical fitness, to a point, is a fine thing, but mental softness is the prime decadence of a healthy civilization.

It is this great principle, learned so early in life, which has generally shaped my quest for the unknown, the meaning of life, and the ultimate purpose and joy of it all.

On the lighter side, with the lake cottage came many years of great pleasure. My mind was just wandering over the many stories that have unfolded at that aquatic paradise. I suppose each one of the topics I have pursued in my quest for the ultimate joy could result is a book itself. However, time and reader interest will not permit more than a casual glance here.

Our place was finished the summer of 1950. I was 12 years old. For many years, the day after school was out in the spring, we would move to the lake until Labor Day in the fall. My father would commute to work a distance of about 38 miles.

This life was pure ecstasy for a youngster. I would rise about 10:00am, eat a hearty breakfast and do any chores I had for the day. At about 11:00am, the group of kids that lived there all summer would meet at the store to plan the day's activities. This group consisted of about thirty rather cosmopolitan young people, and several from smaller towns in the midwest.

Our day would usually consist of tennis for about two hours, then we would head for the beach and play in and out of the water until the evening chill came about 5:00pm. After dinner, we had family and chore time until about 6:30pm, and then back to the store for the evening time youth activities. These were great times!

A person not knowing our group would probably make an assumption here that would lead them down the wrong path of intellectual thought. One might think those evening hours until midnight were filled with sex orgies, carousing, vandalism, alcohol and drugs. Nothing could be further from the truth. The worst thing I remember anyone in the group doing was a game which we preferred to call "Kissie-face." I suppose nowadays it would be called "necking." This game was never played with the girls who were there all summer. There were cottages toward the south end of the lake rented by the week. On Sunday afternoons, our group used to sit at the store waiting to see who would check in. Every rental had to stop at the store. Meanwhile, we would watch all the cars as they waited to register. In this way, we could see all the girls as they came into the resort and check them out as their fathers were checking them in. Thus, now being acquainted, we could start moving in on the girls and draw them into our group by Sunday night of their weeks stay. We played "Kissie-face" with these girls.

As for the activities of the group, most would call them square, but in these square activities, I recall having some of the most fun I believe I ever had. Some nights, parents would let the whole group into their house, and we would play games of Pinochle, Euchre, Hearts, Clue, Monopoly, do card tricks or just sit and talk and munch popcorn. I got so good at Euchre I could make it on a nine and King of Trump. Some nights, we would walk through farmland to the old 19th century graveyard. It was on one of these occasions that I had perhaps one of life's most embarrassing moments.

It was Monday. One of the new girls was a pretty, little, blonde from Chicago. A friend of mine and I had flipped a coin to see who got to date her the first half of the week and who got the rights to the second half. I won the toss.

The group had decided to go back in the hills to the old graveyard that Monday evening, so in the darkness, we swung out the back gate of the resort and into the pasture above. I was walking hand-in-hand with the blonde bombshell. We were walking along the grass area between the plowed furrow and the fence. As anyone familiar with the farm would know the furrow can be anywhere from 6-18 inches deep. I was walking on the furrow side acting the part of the real cool cat, swaggering, and giving my finest male chatter. I was really laying it on thick. On one of my finest remarks and witty anecdotes, I laughed a rakish, sophisticated laugh and turned my head to the wind, whereupon my left foot slipped on the edge of the dew covered furrow, and I fell flat in it.

Now unbeknownst to us there had been cattle grazing in the field that day. I lay there for a couple of seconds very bewildered. For in my hair, on my face, new sweatshirt, and Levi's was the odiferous compound of animal feces. The stench was stifling, overwhelming! The group hooted and held their sides from gales of laughter. I often wonder why we don't take the scriptures literally. It says, "Pride goes before a fall." Talk about a fall! We all ran back to the lake, and I went into the lake clothes and all. Trying to wash the noxious compound off my clothes, I frolicked in the water for several minutes. Emerging from the water, the clothes still repelled the group. The next idea was to drag me behind the launch hoping the moving water across the fabric would loosen the dirt. This also proved to no avail.

Finally, the group expelled me from their presence and I went home. At the rear of the premises, I hatched a daring plan. I stripped off all my clothes, laid them in the swing and ran naked as a jaybird the hundred or so feet into the house.

The soft morning breeze always comes out of the woods east of the house every morning. My mother, rising early, usually raised the east window as she did the morning work at the sink, but this morning the soft flowing zephyrs were not to be. Instead, she got the pungent odor of cow dung. After her investigation, I was aroused rather harshly from my slumber.

One of my morning chores that day was the burying of the clothes.

I never saw the Chicago blonde again.

Those lake days were filled with the finest and most wholesome experiences that a young growing boy could have.

It was here I learned the art of tennis. We had the good fortune one summer of having with us two international tennis stars. They had played several years on the U.S. Davis Cup Team. From them, we learned the basics of tennis and became quite good at the game. It is still quite a thrill to have played with and against a Davis Cup player even though I suspect they carried us in many instances.

Another pursuit of pleasure and the joy of living discovered at the lake was the art of fly-fishing. I first became interested in this form of fishing through a friend of my folks named Sam. He and his wife were quite a friend of the kids and as a result, kids were unafraid to hang around their place even though their children were married and long gone. As it happened, he had an expensive fly rod that he encouraged me to use. I used it regularly to the point where I was better at it than he was.

When I had mastered the use of the fly rod, my dad decided that it would be well for me to have my own. He purchased one for me, and I was out to bag the big ones and bag the big ones I did. It is always quite a thrill to watch the water swoosh and feel the tug of a large blue gill zipping back and forth across in the water. The pole almost bent over double with the fighting weight.

Perhaps even better than that is the joy of fresh fried fish with butter bread and fried potatoes. This meal was always breakfast never any other time of the day. All that grease might kill you if you let it lay in your stomach all night!

One morning it happened. I was coming in the front door of the house and the wind blew the screen door shut before I was ready. The door snapped off the end of my fly rod. I was completely crushed. My father tried his best to fix it and have it fixed, but no one could, so I made the great decision to take my paper route money and invest in a fly rod—the very one I have to this day. I made the trip down to our local sporting good store and planked down on the counter $37.50, a king's ransom for 1952!

My father was always a great still fisherman (cane pole and live bait). I could never see it. Many times I felt guilty about not going fishing with him. Finally early in our lake life, he and I got it out into the open. I told him I just couldn't hack that sitting still and fishing. He understood because he understood me. From then on, he went still fishing and I went fly fishing separately and neither of us felt guilty about not being with the other.

I think there is a lesson to learn here. A father cannot presume to make his son fit into the image of himself, nor can he live his life vicariously in his son by them being buddies or playmates. There is always and should be that distinction of the father-son relationship, where the father is in authority over the son, trying to prepare the son to be independent of him. In short, the minute a child is born, it is the job of the parents to lovingly prepare that child to be independent of them. Anytime a parent does something for a child that he is capable of doing for himself, he does both parties irreparable harm.

One might say that this is cold and rational, but he who says that forgets the word *loving* in the definition. Herein is the key to the whole situation. Inherent in the word *loving* are other ideas like justice, discipline, communication, friendship, obedience, honor, giving, respect, and self-control.

Finally, those lake days lent themselves well to memory because I can remember nothing that was unhappy happening there. The joy of this life at the lake cannot be overstated. Those lovely warm evenings with the group sitting around staring into the campfire, thinking and talking about the life that was lying at our doorstep, led to deep thought and long-standing relationships. We talked freely with one another, and joked and laughed and sang.

A girl, Bev, played the ukulele very well. Many nights we would go down the winding path that led to the point and build a fire on the beach. Here we would lie back on the sand and watch the fire and the stars or study the moon as it rose bright and full over the lake. My parents told me years later that they could hear the strains of a ukulele and young voices singing *Let Me Call You Sweetheart* or *Jada, Jada, Jada, Jada, Jing, Jing, Jing*. Some nights we would push off in canoes and boats for moonlight cruises around the lake singing as we went.

It seemed like just a short time until summer was over and Labor Day was upon us. It was a day spent in taking out the pier, turning off the water, taking down screens and putting up storm windows. It was a day to see the crisp fall beginning, to remember the kids I had met that summer, a day for good intentions of writing to each friend or girl during the winter. It was a sad day, a day of goodbyes—some forever, and some till next spring. It was a day of closing, of finality, and ending. An end to summer with all its carefree living, lost loves, and friendships, an end to no books or teachers or formal learning, an end to green leaves, warm water, waterskis, boats and outdoors.

The geese and ducks that lived at the north end of the lake would nervously await their annual migration in their eternal quest for warm weather. They darted back and forth splashing and honking and agitating one another until some unknown force whispered in every fowl brain, "It's time to go." Then off they would fly in unison using some radar, some guide till the spring came and they would return to the same lake, same stalk, same nest, same activity. Not a whole lot different from me as I got into the car and watched out the back window through tear-filled eyes the geese flying and familiar landmarks disappearing as our car sped back toward home and school on Tuesday morning.

I have learned that permanence of either pleasant or unpleasant things in this life is not a luxury on which the human being can depend.

VIII

Rogers and Ratisbon

"But these pleasures vanish fast
Which by shadows are expressed.
Pleasures are not, if they last:
In their passage is their best.
Glory is most bright and gay
In a flash, and so away."
Samuel Daniel

Tuesday morning after Labor Day came the last year in elementary school, the sixth grade. Gradually, the summer was forgotten as we moved into fall and winter activities.

I, at this time, had a friend who had been my confidant for some years. With him have come some very interesting experiences. His name was Bill Rogers. During this sixth grade time, our country was between wars, so to speak, World War II was over in 1945, but the Korean War was already rumbling into something of great magnitude. It was 1950 and the philosophy in vogue concerning physical education in the schools was geared to making every man a soldier. Thus, we spent most of the time in P.E. practicing drill marching in the gym.

One day in midwinter of that year, Rogers and I were elected to be leaders of the squad. We chanced one day to have a visit from the supervisor of Physical Education in the Belaire Community Schools. Our teacher was talking to the supervisor while Bill and I were at the head of the column. Our teacher was barking out commands to us. At the far end of the gym was a door leading to the boiler room. Down two steps and through the boiler room led to another door at the end of the boiler room to the outside. As the column approached the door at the end of the gym, we were waiting on the left face command. It never came. Mr. Schemerhorn was engrossed in a conversation with the supervisor. Not hearing the command, we went out the boiler room, down the steps, through the back door and across the street. We were almost to Sheridan Park four blocks away when they finally caught up with us.

Then the so-called "Ring Leaders" were summoned into the office of Mr. Tom Krammit, the principal. Upon entering, I knew we were going to be paddled. I saw Mr. Krammit get out his paddle from the closet where he kept his weapons of war.

Mr. Krammit first asked Jack, a "paddle-ees" to bend over and grab his ankles. On the first blow, the paddle broke in half. Bill and I broke into immediate gales of hilarity. This tended to anger the adversary, and he went to his cabinet and brought out what looked like a fraternity paddle and laid three of his hardest whacks on our respective posteriors. Enough said.

*   *   *

At the end of this year, the school held a small graduation ceremony for those of us that were leaving the sixth grade and going on to junior high school. It was during this ceremony, that one of the most bizarre happenings occurred and to this day, I have yet to figure or find out the real truth of the whole affair.

Toward the end of the event, Bill was slated to recite the poem by Robert Browning, *Incident in a French Camp*. Perhaps many readers are familiar with it, but for those who are not, I must repeat this rather short poem.

You know, we French stormed Ratisbon.
A mile or so away,
On a little mound, Napoleon
Stood on our storming-day;
With neck outthrust, you fancy how,
Legs wide, arms locked behind,
As if to balance the prone brow
Oppressive with its mind.

Just as perhaps he mused "My plans
That soar, to earth may fall,
Let once my army-leader Lannes
Waver at yonder wall,"
Out 'twixt the battery smokes there flew
A rider, bound on bound
Full-galloping; nor bridle drew
Until he reached the mound.

Then off there flung in smiling joy,
And held himself erect
By just his horse's mane, a boy:
You hardly could suspect—
(So tight he kept his lips compressed,
Scarce any blood came through
You looked twice ere you saw his breast
Was all but shot in two.)

"Well," cried he, "Emperor, by God's grace
We've got you Ratisbon!
The Marshal's in the market-place,
And you'll be there anon
To see your flag-bird flap his vans
Where I, to heart's desire,
Perched him!" The chief's eye flashed; his plans
Soared up again like fire.

The chief's eye flashed; but presently
Softened itself, as sheathes
A film the mother-eagle's eye
When her bruised eaglet breathes;
"You're wounded!" "Nay," the soldier's pride
Touched to the quick, he said:
"I'm killed, Sire!" And, his chief beside,
Smiling, the boy fell dead.

On the last line, this poem says the following line, "and smiling
the boy fell dead". At this point, Bill fell off the stage on which he
was standing, hitting his head on the concrete floor. He fell a distance
of about five-and-a-half feet. He lay still for a few minutes, and then
jerked like a nervous muscular disorder or even a fit of sorts was

overtaking him. The school called an ambulance immediately. Bill lay quiet with his eyes closed, and many thought him to be dead.

While waiting for the ambulance, I leaned over his still body and whispered his name. He opened his left eye, and winked knowingly at me and said nothing. He stayed in the hospital for two days.

I have asked him many times since, but he dismisses the whole subject by, "You'll never know, will you?" I still don't know if the ruin of the whole ceremony, the stir of the entire group of parents, the two days in the hospital, the examination by school officials and doctors, was one gigantic put-on or not.

IX

Mens Sano in Corpore Sang

"Bodily exercise profitith little."
Saint Paul

It is curious phenomenon of our culture that the male members of our society who have trained their muscles and ligaments to perform with agility and quickness, a non-essential and time-wasting activity, are elevated to the standard of some Caesar or conquering lord home from a campaign in Persia. The casual observer would read sour grapes into the above thought. However, I think I can speak with some authority.

As mentioned earlier, I excelled at tennis playing in both high school and college. I played junior league hockey and high school basketball. I also played varsity football in high school and varsity baseball. I was not excellent, but rather good at the bulk of these sports. Therefore, the sour grape pointing of the finger, I believe, is unjustified.

I think there is something sick about a society that pays a million dollars to a man for throwing an oblong ball accurately or putting a round ball through a hoop, and only $30,000 or so to the discoverer of a cure for polio or measles.

Don't be mistaken, I think pro athletes should be paid. I enjoy immensely coming home from church on Sunday and relaxing while the BlackHawks wipe out Montreal. It is not the concept of the whole thing to which I object. It is the emphasis on winning and the supernaturality of the performers that I have the greatest objection. Just because a person throws a small leather ball to another person, this does not give him wisdom, knowledge, or super human tendencies. Immediately, when a person becomes a "Star", he is an expert on every subject from soup to nuts. What astounds me even further is that gullible people accept what he says as revelation without even checking it out. The impression on the young and immature is even more staggering.

The idea of winning is a good one under controlled circumstances, but I don't think we can justify winning at all costs under any circumstances. I think we have lapsed into a pseudo-psychology that says that the making of a man or building character is inherent in the bruising, crushing and killing of the opposing individual on his way to the goal of the win. If a game can be played for the fun or thrill of it, and while playing you desire highly the goal of winning, in my judgment, this is acceptable, but the philosophy, "Winning isn't everything, it's the only thing" has led us down the primrose path of barbarism. I have been down this road in search of the ultimate thrill, it just isn't there.

As I entered junior high school, I met a physical education teacher and coach who was destined to have an influence on my life. One of my biggest hopes was to play basketball, to be a star, to go the route of glory. The hope was there, the ability was there, the practice was there, all seemed to be on my side. I went into junior high as the best player in the new group of seventh graders. We put together quite a team. I was at guard for both years and accumulated enough points for four varsity letters. Larger than most of the youngsters at that age, the sport was fun and exciting.

It was here that I met Bennie Burton, the mentor of the program. He was a tall, athletic man with a lot of potential. He was not destined to stay in junior high long. He put together this squad and took us to the finals of the city tournament. I learned a lot from him and basketball was the least of the knowledge. Already, I was formulating the idea that the glory, the thrill, the ultimate purpose was not in athletics. However, the main points I learned from him were his attributes of quiet authority, knowledge of the game, zest for living, and a fighting spirit, to go on and never give up.

He had drive and what we termed as "guts." He was not one to think that while he was at this job, he was just filling in time. Rather he told us that while he was here, we were going to have the best team, the best school and the best time ever. All of us liked him immensely. If he would have picked up the flag and said follow me boys, we would have followed him into most any fray.

Burton, as we respectfully called him, made a statement rather in passing that I perhaps will never forget. "Boys," he said, "Give me a man with average ability, willing to work, not counting the sacrifice and I'll send him to the top of everything he tries. Confidence and hard work are 60% of the game."

We lost the final game of the city championship, not because of lack of confidence or hard work, but in that remaining 40% are mixed together a combination of ability and luck. We were ahead by 1 point going into the last forty seconds. We had the ball and were working in a semi-slowdown, waiting for a good, last shot. The opposition was pressing at the time-line. Tom sent the ball accurately to Hilie under the bucket, and he was to get an easy lay-up for the ice bucket. Hilie couldn't find the handle and traveled with the ball. Four seconds left and they had the ball at the backcourt baseline. Our opponents threw it in bounds in the foul lane and their little guard threw a baseball shot the full length of the court. We watched the ball sail over the center circle as the gun sounded. We stood in disbelief and our hearts sunk as the brown, shining spheroid ripped the chords, hung momentarily in the net, and dropped silently to the floor.

We were stunned, immobilized, completely without the use of our senses. It is my feeling that defeat, a good, solid, just defeat can either bring out the best or the worst in a man. Burton set the tone, as any coach can and should do. He came into the locker room holding the runner-up trophy and a big, smile on his face. He knew we had given it everything we had and had fought to the last ditch. Now it was over, it was just a game, and we lost. He then took us all down to Roco's restaurant and we had a "victory" celebration. There were no long faces or post-mortems. We ate and had a great time. We were not celebrating a loss, but rather we were celebrating life and our ability to give our best to it. I then began to realize that defeat was an opportunity to grow and mature. Also and perhaps more importantly, it was such a small part of the total life picture, and it should be treated that way.

This would, I think, lead us to the conclusion once again that my father had reached, and I was beginning to grasp. Most happenings in our life of are such small consequence taken individually that we must be careful not to overrate them. However, one should be careful to spot trends or groups of experiences that point up what is happening in a life.

I am here saying if I would have taken that one defeat as a way of life, an attitude, then it would be an indication of something seriously wrong in my life and thinking. Most human beings have a tendency to drift aimlessly and are undisciplined. To them, the philosophy of small events being inconsequential, would be disastrous. This happens mainly because they lack the discipline of the will and insight to introspect.

X

Nemo Liber Est Qui Corpori Servit

He bowed his head, and bent his knee
Upon the monarch's silken stool;
His pleading voice arose: "O Lord,
Be merciful to me, a fool."
Edward R. Sill

Off hand, I can't remember who said it, but whoever did, was majestic in his sweep of adolescence. "Isn't it unfortunate that youth is wasted on the young?" Those years 'twixt 12 and 20, how can we ever dare to describe them? What similes or metaphors could describe that euphoric feeling of such intense loves and hates? What verb could we use to present the look that young girl gave you across the schoolroom? How can we describe the tingle and explosions in your brain when you brushed the hand or hair of that young fem? Or who could write a word that says I think you're something special or I care about you?

These are the first impulses of man's first few hints of lust. Left to bloom unchecked, it blossoms into the hideous flower of disgust, dirt and vileness. Here is a question so often asked by many of us. What happens to that beautiful feeling of love, tenderness, that tingle we were talking about earlier? What happens as those wonderful, good feeling gives way to lust, premarital sex, incest, fornication, adultery, perversion, and all heinous sins of the flesh?

Most assuredly the answer lies in God's answer, "The heart is deceitful and desperately wicked . . . in sin did my mother conceive me, . . . all have sinned and have turned every one to his own way, . . .

---

there is none righteous, no not one." Jesus said you must be born again; you must have this basic nature with which you were born, changed.

These are the same questions I was asking as those first hints of something happening inside my body were awakening. Here is another use, not only of Christian principles, but of discipline and self-control. I would even say discipline and self-control are part of Christian principles.

The evening after the basketball defeat, a party was held at school to honor the team. I walked into this party as the swaggering, conquering hero. I quickly spotted the girl in whom I happened to interested at the time. She was talking to a group of her girlfriends over by the jukebox. Our eyes met across the room, and she jiggled and giggled nervously. I slowly worked my way through the mob of people across the room, slowed by receiving the congratulations of some friends and teachers. This was good, however, because you never want to seem too eager to the girl of the moment.

There seems to be an unwritten code among girls, for as I approached, the other four girls disappeared. There she was, Judy, a vision of beauty, loveliness and budding femininity. We waltzed out to the dance floor and danced the next several dances, holding each other as if one of us would get away. The party was a huge success. I say this with tongue in cheek knowing that the party would have been a success no matter what was going on. We could have held it in the black hole of Calcutta and still be successful. It was the frame of mind that made it a success. There is a good point for children and youth workers. We danced, played games, ate, drank and got our letters and trophies. All that I do not recall very well; I don't even know where my letters are today.

What I do recall was the ride home from the party. I was riding in the back seat with Judy; her mom and dad were in the front seat. We were talking softly about the nice party and the good time we had, when the conversation took the following bent.

I: You really are a good dancer.

She: So are you.

I: I think this has been one of the nicest weeks of my life.

She: For me too. I watched you play more than anybody.

I: Why?

She: Because we kind of like each other, don't we?

I: Yes, I think you're neat.

She: You're pretty wonderful yourself.

Then softly, with our faces close together, we passed under a street light. The light flickered across her face to reveal her eyes slightly open and red lips soft and luscious looking.

She: Kiss me!

A few seconds later, I opened my eyes and saw familiar landmarks coming into view. We rumbled up in front of my house, and I said thank you to her parents and jumped out. I never touched the sidewalk all the way to the porch! I heard the violins playing, saw the stars twinkling and the moon winking.

The crisp February snow was bright with the moonlight as I looked out my bedroom window that night. I must have sat there for an hour just studying and thinking. I was happy, thrilled, and yet in the back of my mind was that nagging doubt that had dogged my steps for years. Wasn't there certainly more to life than this thrill that was already beginning to pass?

The immature might be thinking I was in love with this girl. The first love how sweet it is. Nonsense! Love wasn't within a thousand miles. It was lust, pure and simple. Unfortunately, what most people call love is really lust. This is the reason why it crumbles and dies. Love can never die; God is love.

After much thought, I faced squarely the situation. What was it that I really wanted with this girl? It was lust alright!!! Once faced, I really never had much trouble with lust again. You see the thought process goes something like this. I faced my desires straight out and saw that it was lust. Then, once seeing what it really was, it became a matter of the will. Since lust was repugnant to my basic set of values, it became a rather simple thing to see where lust would lead. Once the end result was seen, it then became a matter of the will to control one's basic tendencies. Thus, the fact of flirting with or courting became a game to play since the end or control was on my side and in my favor. I could very easily turn on and off my emotions at will. I became very good at the game and practiced considerably.

So, it is easy for one to see that I transferred the desire from the object to the thrill of playing the game. The game was intoxicating, and I was very much in demand. Many the girl who evidently thought I was playing hard to get, because I was literally pure as the driven snow. Actually, it wasn't so much of hard to get, but a combination of my basic principles of purity that I had been taught, and the knowledge of life's ruin caused by easy virtue.

Love—Never, not under these circumstances. Love is another, whole different ball game. Love has ideas of totally giving, maturity, duty, discipline, growing together, friendship, companionship, childrearing, cooperation, financial planning, religious beliefs, and a myriad of other small, daily compromises.

Love—Absurd. However, I am shocked as I have talked to literally thousands of young people about it. Many have mentioned that their idea of love is based upon the foolishness of an incident like that which I have just recounted. In fact, many have based a marriage on just such foolish premises or a biological commitment, which is equally as foolish.

Most things passing under the disguise of love are just uncontrolled biological drives of immature persons.

Love—Not in your wildest dreams. This is insatiable lust born of an unregenerate heart.

WHO CAN KNOW TRUE LOVE?

XI

White is Beautiful

Whose woods these are I think I know.
His house is in the village though
He will not see me stopping here
To watch his woods fill up with snow.
Robert Frost

Several years ago, I was traveling in my car south of Indianapolis, Indiana. I was alone in the car listening to a radio. It was before Christmas and the announcer was describing a little vignette about himself. He was saying that he was at "The Circle" in downtown Indianapolis. The choirs were singing Christmas carols, the snow was blowing and accumulating, and the children were playing. He went on to describe this rather idyllic scene in some great detail, and I was rather enthralled by his description.

Then he went on to say that he was humming a Christmas carol as he walked and his boots were rustling in the new fallen snow, but the next words he said were spoke were in a low, raspy voice.

"Then I got in my car!!!"

With him, the joy of the idyllic scene seemed to disappear when he started driving in the slush, the snow, the crud which we call winter.

When the leaves have all dropped, and the days have shortened and the clouds have rolled in from the west unendingly, we know in this latitude that earth is trying to prepare us for the onslaught of winter.

When viewed in the right perspective, winter, I think, is one of our best climatic times.

Winter has always been one of my times when security has been at its height. It is a time for families to grow closer, to renew old friendships around a fire, to realize that we need one another. For winter is a time when nature seems to ask of us our every fiber and sinew.

In my days of adolescence, winter brought my favorite sports: hockey, sledding and pleasure skating. Later on, snowmobiling and motorcycle sledding became part of the winter liturgy. Who can describe those cold, crisp mornings after a new snowfall of perhaps 8-10 inches. I would sit around the radio intently listening for the announcement that school was closed for the day. Once this precious announcement came, my brother would shut off the radio and prepare for the day.

The day's preparation would be a hardy breakfast and then bundling in heavy clothing to beat the chill of sub-freezing temperatures. We would fling our skates over our shoulder, pick up our sticks and a puck and head for the woods behind our house. Early in the fall, we would dam up a little creek running through the field and let it flood a small area of the field north of the woods. Then as winter would come, this area would become an excellent skating area, sheltered nicely by the woods and slightly lower than the rest of the terrain. We would spend the entire day back there.

Upon reaching the rink, we would first have to push the snow off. We pushed the "shovels" across the ice. These "shovels" were not really shovels but two pieces of wood nailed to a third piece of 1x8 which served as a plow. One person would get between the two pieces, put one hand on each piece and push and skate. This worked like a snowplow. In short order, the rink was cleared. We usually marked the rink with red paint early in the season then carefully covered it with water and let it freeze over.

In our neighborhood, we had the good fortune of having 31 boys between ages 10 and 17 (at that time). We had no lacking for players and skaters. Usually the girls were allowed to skate on the west side of the pond, but if we had too many fellows, we would make two rinks and have two games going at once. The girls would have to move elsewhere or play with us, which they did not want to do. The reason being, when someone got into the game, they were treated alike. This discouraged the girls somewhat.

I remember several occasions that I played for several hours without too much of a break. I was so thirsty that I thought I was going to die. In fact, the entire group was parched. The group all skated over to the edge of the pond where we had chopped a hole in the ice and there we drank the icy water. It was delicious!

This activity would come to a screeching halt at 3:00pm when several of us would mount our bicycles and head for the paper corner.

At that time (1950), my brother and I had the largest paper route in Belaire, about 300 customers. The paper truck, (*Sentinel*, always the *Sentinel*), would drop the bundles around 3:15pm. The process of folding then began. The fold would have to be tight enough for me to throw the paper a distance of 30 to 60 feet. My brother threw backhand, and I threw forehand. We would go in the same direction on opposite sides of the street. We had the route so divided that we could cover the whole route without doubling back or crossing each other's tracks.

At the end of the run, we would all meet at Rudy's Store between Sheean and McMann Streets. The real thrill came to be a game called "Who can get there first." Rudy even participated by usually giving some kind of a treat to the winner each evening.

Several nights I can remember flinging papers so hard and quickly that milk bottles were broken, papers on porch roofs, and even broken storm doors. *The Sentinel* usually split the cost of the repairs with us. This kept us from becoming too careless as part of the money was coming out of our pockets.

It certainly is a fine thing that time does so much to heal the wounds of memory. Right now, I have a good pleasant feeling as I look back on those days, but somewhere in the back of my brain, I see myself on the verge of tears as my bicycle lay in a heap with 150 papers strewn about in the mud, rain and snow . . . or delivering past the Mazzoties as Al and Lugi would sit in their bedroom window with BB guns peppering me as I came by . . . or the vicious fights with the Von Druken boys on newspaper corner.

I learned not to be too afraid of dogs as I did the paper route business. I gained confidence as I battled them on their own terrain. I remember one outing with a black male Spaniel with red eyes. I had just missed a porch on Sheean Street. When I stopped at the next house, out of the bushes roared this gigantic black dog. He jumped at me about chest high, but I blocked him by cracking him over the head with the large rolled paper I was carrying. He dropped to the ground somewhat stunned, and I kicked him in the head with my large heavy boot (some might remember them being called "clod hoppers"). I now had the dog in my power. I booted him another couple of times to show him who was boss and then continued my rounds. I was the first one at Rudy's that night.

Thursday night always offered many surprises to the unwitting paperboy, especially in winter. Cold, Thursday, winter evenings were a time to endure much pain and suffering—collections. I would start out collecting my half of the route. My brother and I devised an ingenious plan for handling complaints. We had our books set up so that we would collect the opposite half of what we delivered. During collection, as a complaint would arise we would simply, honestly say, "Well, I don't deliver this area so I can't really answer your complaint." This usually sufficed because the complaints were of such a nature they were easily forgotten by both, complainer and defendant. Sometimes, we would be out till 9:30pm or so on those dark, cold winter evenings. Many times my gloves froze to the rings on the collection book. If I couldn't move my fingers enough to tear off the little tags, then I would ask the patron to tear them off for me.

It is always interesting to note the lengths that people go to avoid a kid collecting 50¢. Many times, I would knock on a door to collect and see supposedly grownup, mature people, crawling on their hands and knees out the back door to the garage, or I would see them hide behind curtains at the window, or snap off all the lights at my knock. I have yet to understand this kind of behavior.

Some people would actually use this kind of behavior at Christmas time because they felt obligated to give me a tip for Christmas, and they didn't feel they could or wanted to. Laying these things aside, Christmas was a fine time of year for the paperboy. On our route, I would get as high as $85 and many boxes of candy and goodies the collection night before Christmas. I always carried my large paper bag just for bringing home the loot. I ate quite well for a few weeks!

Technically, I was on salary and my brother was on commission. I worked for him on a straight $3 per week arrangement. Some weeks, he would make 50¢ or a $1, but at the beginning of the month when the good customers were paying for the entire month, he could make as high as $40. On average, he made about $6-10 per week. It was good money for those days, and I had many of the niceties that others did not have.

The only requirement my father put on the money earned was to have final veto on its dispersal. He had told me that he was not going to make his boys "turn their money home" like he had done till his 21st birthday. From his remarks, this evidently was a requirement that chafed his neck while growing. Ours was kind of a political arrangement somewhat like Congress passing appropriations bills and the President vetoing or signing them. Not often did my father use his veto power. I can't recall whether this was because I was a good budgeter or he was permissive, (but I don't recall him ever being really permissive.)

All this high finance came to an end the winter of 1951. Under mutual agreement, my brother and I decided to dissolve the partnership. He was working as a carry-out at Johnson's Market, and I was trying the glory of a basketball career. We decided the paper route business was obsolete, but it was a little hard showing the new kid the ropes of the route which I had put so much of myself.

Every so often, I drive past that old corner and in my mind's eye, I see myself sitting folding papers and putting them in the news bag. When I see that picture, I feel so sorry for myself. My heart aches as I think of that little kid trying to make something of himself. So ignorant, so frail of mind, so unsophisticated, so open, so friendly, not cynical or sarcastic. Isn't it a shame youth is wasted on the young?

XII

Amicus Est Tanquam Alter Idem

Come, poor remains of friends, rest on this rock.
Shakespeare

Some afternoon when you are bored or if you are lacking for conversation at a party, try the following bit of conversation and you are sure to have goldmines of provocative chatter. You will also be thrown out with the garbage. Ask a person (any person) how many friends he has. After he tells you, then ask him how he knows? With this conversation, you will literally hear thousands of definitions of friendship and more defensive noise than perhaps you've ever heard.

It has been my experience the more a person defends his "friends", the less of a friend he really is. My hypotheses: Whom most people define as friends are really acquaintances.

This game is really fun to play with my students about age 15. To children of this age, the gregarious factor is so important, but they are too immature to realize that it isn't important at all. The peer pressure of this group is astounding! It is most amusing and sometimes tragic to watch the adolescent mind at work as they struggle to play at adulthood. Youth are the most transparent fakes in the world. Except for the obvious disarray of personality, one can predict their dialogue almost word-for-word. A youth seems to be so idealistic and perceptual. These attributes, though perhaps present, are highly overrated. Most of youth's idealism and justice is rooted in selfishness and immaturity.

Should one dare to point their finger at me and say I am cutting or hacking away at youth and their priorities and perspectives, the answer would be yes, but perhaps not in the way the pointer might think. I take this position not from malice or prejudice because I like these kids immensely! Rather, I take this position from rational observation of children during my twenty-year tenure as an instructor. Second and perhaps most important to this narrative, I draw from vast experiences as I, too, passed through this perilous river of adolescence. It is with this second position in mind that I launch into the discussion of friends and the role that they play in the development of ones search for the ultimate of life's possibilities.

Was it Aeschylus that said, "For a man to have more than two friends in a lifetime, he is either a god or a liar"? I have had literally thousands of acquaintances, but only a handful of friends.

It might be well at this point to put up some guideposts or some limits of this subject. What must the atmosphere be like for the seed of friendship to even germinate, let alone grow or blossom? First, a person must be on the same socio-economic level. The old story of Prince Charming coming out of the gleaming white castle on a snow-white charger dressed in magnificent clothes to the ghetto hovels below is asinine. This simply cannot happen in any lasting relationship. The differences are too great for their relationship to bear the storm of years of different preparation for their lifestyles. This odd couple arrangement makes entertaining theatre-fare, but most assuredly could not harmonize in natural life.

A psychologist acquaintance once told the story of a couple that shows this lifestyle difference on a very low level. It seems that the mister wanted the toilet paper to roll from off the top and the misses wanted it to roll off the bottom. Each would change the paper every time they were in the bathroom. This became such a bone-of-contention with them they finally came near divorce over this seeming incompatibility. If this relationship could not sustain the stress of this rather insignificant difference of lifestyle, how much less could a person of widely differing social and economic background hope to sustain a relationship.

Second, two people basically must come from the same intellectual and educational background. The depth of conversation of eighth grade graduate and college graduate must of necessity be limited, if by no other factor than vocabulary. Please be not mistaken, I have in no way stated that one is more honorable than the other, or one person is better or more honorable. What I am saying is that the probability of the two having anything is common or having mutually discussable items is practically zero.

Third, for two people to have any lasting relationship, they must agree on their philosophical convictions. I prefer to call them religious convictions. If I am to believe the Scriptures, which I most assuredly do, than I can see no way for anyone to have a permanent relationship with anyone who does not have the same spiritual convictions. It is just not in the cards.

Let me expound on these religious convictions, though, lest someone misinterpret what I mean. Many times, Christians have argued over peripheral Scriptural matters never knowing quite God's intention. A friend of mine and I used to go round and round over Arminianism versus Calvinism, neither one of us convincing the other. We closed this chapter in our lives knowing that on this side of eternity, we would never fully have the answer to this thorny problem. There are several areas where men, great scholarly men of God, have studied entire lifetimes on these debatable questions. My point is this: the things I believe God has wanted to impress indelibly on our minds, He has told us repeatedly in no uncertain language or tone. The Ten Commandments are a good example of these straight forward "Thou shalt" or "Thou shalt not" declarations from Almighty God.

Here is the case in point. God has spoken in his Word in many different kinds of descriptions about this very point. He has said, "What fellowship has light with darkness?" "Be not unequally yoked together with unbelievers." "You must choose God or mammon." "No man can serve two masters." "You are in the world but not of the world." "I send you forth as sheep among wolves, as lambs to the slaughter." The scriptures substantiate this third point so clearly. Two people cannot possibly have a relationship with one another unless this qualification has been satisfied. We cannot go into any relationship, friendship, fellowship or even world harmony without this basic requirement, I do not believe.

In other words, one can go no farther in any relationship, be it marriage or friendship (hopefully both) until common spiritual ground has been established. This should be done early, VERY EARLY, in the relationship. If a person is thinking of marriage, it should be established <u>BEFORE</u> the first date. Here is the point at which most Christian young people falter. They seem to think they can flirt with danger and moral decay by being friends with the world and with people who have never experienced the miracle of regeneration. It is simply impossible to date or hang around "non-born-again professing Christians" and live the Christian life. In fact, if a person makes this kind of contact a constant habit, the Scriptures attest that their Salvation is suspect.

That is, they are just playing at Christianity and probably have never been born-again themselves.

With these three prerequisites met (Socio-economic level, education/intellectual level, Religious convictions), there is a possibility that friendship might occur.

XIII

Birds of a Feather

"He was my friend, faithful and just to me."
Shakespeare

My life has always been one of many social contacts and very few involvements with people or organizations. I have never been a joiner. I always felt that I should lead and have other people join. The thought of me joining someone else's group without my organization and leadership was ridiculous. Therefore, commitments to causes and people were few and far between.

Early in life I chanced upon a person who was to be a real confidant. He was a fine pal and buddy. Bill Rogers was a chunky kid of jolly personality and intellectual mind. Bill and I were great pals. You met him in an earlier chapter falling off the stage of the elementary school. You will meet him again later as I wend my way through high school. Therefore, I'll let him leave and call on him later to testify concerning his part in my quest for the ultimate meaning or reason for my existence.

Of the two adults that really influenced my life, other than my folks, the reader has already met one, Bennie Burton. The other was a man named Harvey Higgins. I first met Harvey on a rather casual basis when he and his family came to our church just after the war. I met him officially later after a rather traumatic experience. I am referring to an experience of long duration climaxing in a rather large run-in with my parents.

In the earlier years at Sunday School, I was taught by Godly elderly women whom I did not appreciate until much later in life. My class was a particularly unruly one with very little respect for the church or our lovely teachers. Two of the ladies had nervous breakdowns and were in bed almost two months. I think the basic cause of one of the breakdowns was the plugging of the stools in the men's restroom. All the toilets were flushed and water was running through two of the Sunday School rooms in the basement, one of which was hers. This was a trifle disconcerting to ladies of such social prominence and genteel upbringing.

The class was then presented with a male teacher who presently tried to get us into shape. Alas, his efforts were to no avail. He retired to tranquilizers and bed rest. Then the class was moved to the vestibule of the church next to the class of most of the parents of the boys in class. The parents were notified of the complete situation and attended their class sitting close to the separating wall. This quieted the class into a truce with the instructor.

It is at this point that God, working through the Church Council, asked one of the young Deacons, Harvey Higgins, to assume the leadership of our obstreperous class. He accepted under the following conditions:

1. The class was to be moved to the basement storeroom next to the boiler room.
2. No interference from the parents or the church council.
3. A minimum of 18 months to get the job done.
4. Freedom to use facilities and methods to win the boys' favor and respect.

Thus came the first Sunday that the new regime took over. The group was all marshaled along the lower basement under the sanctuary, past the plumbing and electricity controls, back under the organ pipes and compressor, then finally into the small storeroom that had been cleared away of junk for this occasion.

Harv was waiting for us in a new, brown suit with small, black pin stripes, brown tie and light beige shoes. He was about 5' 10", 170 pounds with black hair and glasses. He was also just fresh out of the service from the European theater of WWII. His athletic frame was honed to a fine edge in great physical shape. Harv had dark eyes that peered through small slits in his eyelids. He eyed each one of us as we entered.

My cousin Ben and I were the last two to enter the small cubicle. We sat together near the light switch to the windowless room. The door was closed and we all waited to see what kind of person this was going to be. I watched Ben closely as he leaned back on the hind two legs of his chair, his head very close to the light switch. I kept the corner of my eye on Ben's hands as he clasped them over his head in a semi-relaxed listening style. Ever closer, his clasped hands felt the smoothness of the wall. I just caught it out of my right eye as Ben's hands were on the switch. Then . . . Total and complete darkness!!! Everybody was hollering and yelling when the lights came back on. Harv was standing by the switch, one hand still on it. I looked at the chair where Ben had been sitting; he was not there! My eyes cast about the room till they rested in the far corner which had been stacked high with old rags and clothes. Ben was lying in the corner with blood running from his mouth and nose. The left side of his face was ruby red where blood had was brought to the skin's surface. Harv said not a word but went right on with the lesson. Needless to say, we were in rapt attention.

There was only one other occasion early in his teaching career that bears any significance here. Jerry, a rather stocky kid of immense strength for his age, questioned Harv's authority. Harv picked him up literally by the collars of his suit coat and slammed him against the wall. Jerry hit the wall and slid down it dazed to the floor. Things only got better from this point on.

For the most part, in three Sundays Harv had the entire class seated and in attention. He then proceeded to work on our mental and spiritual behavior and attitudes. He had conquered the physical, but the mental and spiritual took long hours of prayer, love, and companionship. Let youth workers and ministers take an important lesson here. Very little seems to be done by God or man to the mental or spiritual portion of young people until their bodies have been disciplined and quieted. I had great times with Harv and the others, but always I knew where the boundaries lay. It was from these experiences that I learned to honor, respect and hallow the House of God. This rarely, I fear, is taught today.

We discussed, both individually and as a group, some of life's most important topics. Several times on Sunday evening after church, I would be talking to Harv about a hangup at school or the like, and he would say, "Go tell your folks I'll bring you home". We would then go out to Roco's or some other drive-in to eat and talk. It was this kind of love and caring that so endeared him to each one of us. He really cared what happened to us and we knew it. Not by telling us, but his actions, life, and deeds spoke clearly the message he was saying with his mouth.

A funny thing happened as I was to leave this class at the end of the year. I walked into the next year's class with the rest of my peers and there was Harv waiting for us. He taught our class from the 8th grade until we went off to college!

Harv was a businessman in Belaire. Thus, he had the where-with-all to have fun as well as spiritual rejuvenation. I went to hockey games, baseball games in Chicago, softball games, boating, water and snow skiing—you name it and we did it. I grew to love that man and for that which he stood. I remember especially a night when a special speaker from Mansfield, Ohio was speaking at our church. For some unknown reason after the service, I was crying profusely. Ben and I were in the upper fellowship hall, and I felt so badly not for myself but for Ben. I felt like a gigantic heavy weight was about my neck in sorrow for him. I went to Harv and he came and talked to Ben for a long time. I left and never quite knew the outcome of that confrontation with spiritual maturity.

I was moving faster toward the goal of spiritual commitment. I was beginning to feel the breath of the Hound of Heaven as He came closer and closer to my heart, my life, my all.

XIV

Blood is Thicker than Water

Howe'er blind Fortune turn her giddy wheel.
Michael Drayton

During the time of my early spiritual rebellion, my comrade in arms was my cousin, Ben. Ben was fun loving and intelligent, two qualities needed to survive the rigors of my companionship.

We hung together like thieves those early years of junior high and freshmen year. I spent time at his house with his family and he spent much time at my place. I think we were friends even though I have not seen him in twenty years. He fulfilled most of the requirements for friendship.

I felt a special kind of affection for him as he, at that time had passed through one life crisis and was in the midst of another. Some four years earlier, just after the war, his father was killed in a plane crash. Now, in his formative junior high years, his sister was dying of a terminal kidney disease. His mother had remarried and the family was in transition. Ben was ripe for rebellion and teenage problems. I think maybe my family can take part of the credit that the problems were not more hostile.

One Sunday evening, Ben and I were sitting in the balcony to the left of the pulpit area. The church service had the good fortune of having a virtuoso soprano singer for the special music that evening. She was singing her lungs out with arias, cadenzas, and the like in a loud operatic voice. Ben turned to me and loud enough for me to hear over the racket said, "Somebody throw that seal a herring fish." On the words, "Somebody throw" the soprano came to a "Grande Pause" and stopped dead short. The silence was deafening; all that was heard was Ben's voice ringing throughout the entire church. I was deeply embarrassed, and I am sure Ben felt badly twice.

During the seemingly dull sermons, Ben and I would write wild commercials designed to sell unusual products. Paper was a hard commodity to come by so we used the visitor cards in the pews. (Incidentally, I'm sure many of the church hoped that we would use the cards legitimately.) I particularly remember one difficult item for which to write a commercial. Ben and I were trying to write a commercial for the sale of a fur-lined bathtub. The possibilities were endless and some of the descriptions were perhaps even crude.

Every Saturday night our church would rent the gym of our church's college, located across the street from our church. I would, along with my brother, play basketball there each week. Harv was the mentor and head honcho of the entire program.

One Saturday night in December, we arrived at the gym only to find the gym doors locked and bolted. We were immediately incensed. Ben and I proceeded to go home and write a terse letter to the church council. One must keep in mind that my father and Harv were both deacons and members of the church council. We sent the letter to the council never talking to either of the two closest people we knew best. Both my father and Harv were unpleasantly surprised when this letter was brought up on the agenda. I was rather soundly chewed out for this oversight of common courtesy.

I learned a powerful lesson from this—a lesson which most people learn by experience but sometimes too late to really matter. It is not so much what you know or how much you know, but who you know that can help in a solution to problems. Usually, the best results are made working through the normal channels—those people that know you best. These are the ones that work the hardest for you.

* * *

In the early days of television, Sid Caesar was the reigning king. On his old show with Carl Reiner, Howard Morris, Imogene Coca and later, Nannette Fabray, he used to do a sketch called "Cool Cees". In this sketch, he played the part of a hippie saxophone-playing musician. The punch lines were superlative and highly imaginative. Every Wednesday morning after Sid Caesar, each of us would talk, digest, and rehash the entire program. I could hardly wait to get to school and ask the boys what they liked or enjoyed most.

Ben and I got so involved in it that we finally wrote a script in which Edward R. Murrow was interviewing Cool Cees. The characters were take-offs of those on the Caesar show, but the script was purely out of our imagination. We were so eager to play our script that we decided to give it a quick run-through before church started one Sunday. In those days, I, along with Ben, Jerry, and Jim, had a bad habit of spending the time of the morning service in the Radio Room of the church. This room had a one-way window so that from the radio room one could see the congregation, but the congregation could not see into the room. We had decided to put the "Cool Cees" sketch on tape since the facilities were all there in the Radio Room. I played the part of Edward R. Murrow and Ben played the part of "Cool Cees". We laughed and giggled our way through the entire sketch. I could hardly wait to hear the tape. We urged Jim to put the tape on and play it, for we could not postpone our excitement any longer. Jim deftly put the tape on and started to play it. I was standing by the window enraptured with the sound of my own voice. I was chuckling and giggling when I chanced to look out the window at the congregation. My face turned ashen and my heart skipped a beat. The audience was looking at one another, and the pastor standing at the podium was looking up toward the Radio Room. I immediately sensed that Jim not only let us hear the tape, but also plugged the tape into the public address system. The entire congregation was hearing this tape as the pastor was preaching!

For an instant, I was paralyzed, and then caught sight of my father. Ben, Jim, and Jerry and I pulled the plug on everything, including the address system and did what every red-blooded teenager would have done. WE RAN LIKE A THIEF IN THE NIGHT, out the door, down the back stairs, into the alley and flat out to the drugstore at the corner of Fulton and Sheean. There I waited for the guillotine to fall. Some twenty minutes later, I saw my father walking thoughtfully toward the drug store. He walked in, spotted me, and strode over, but did not say a word. He put his hand on my shoulder, and I thought he was going to touch his index finger and thumb together through the larger muscle on my shoulder and neck . . . He did. I was in terrible pain, but he still did not speak the first word.

I got into the backseat where my brother was sitting holding back a silly smirk. He then proceeded into an act that is quickly discernable to anyone who has grown up in a sibling relationship. Half whispering and giggling, he was gesturing with his hands those famous words we all know and have heard so often from our brothers and sisters. Quote, "Boy, are you going to get it." Over and over again, he quietly reiterated this warning. He quickly stopped this nonsense when my father reached around with his right hand and clipped my brother on the leg. Dad turned into the driveway and still not a word spoken from either of my parents. My mother told me to go to my room and not come out until my father came up. I stayed in my room all afternoon waiting for the tell-tale steps coming up the stairs. JUDGMENT HAD COME.

I was expecting the worst, anything from a spanking to a yelling. I got neither. Dad sat down on the edge of the bed and beckoned me to sit next to him. All he said was, "This morning I was very, very sorry that we were both party to that scene. You have damaged both of us immeasurably. I was very, very disappointed in you." A whipping could not have cut me any deeper. I was crushed. I knew that my actions had not only hurt my father, but had cast a dark cloud over my own budding reputation.

XV

The American Dream

The sheepskin: I turned it, I twist it,
I caressed it, I kist it.
Self

For centuries, precious, chosen few were selected somehow by the fates to enter into a small, elite group called the educated. During these centuries, man struggled with the grossest of problems: ignorance, illiteracy, and barbarism. Then, in rapid succession, the Renaissance, Reformation, and Industrial Revolution forced sleeping humanity into action.

The Renaissance, I suspect, only affected the ruling or princely class, but in affecting them, ideas were beginning to germinate for all mankind. In my judgment, the Reformation took the openness of the Renaissance and translated it to man's need, mainly the reading of the Word of God in his own language. Thus, spurred on to read, the education of the common man was a short step. The last giant nail in the coffin of ignorance was put in place. The Industrial Revolution forced the common man to get in step or be left staring at the rich factory gate. True, the injustice of sweatshops, child labor, and all the objects of the famous British Labor Laws were still left to die a slow death, but the seed of education was planted and certainly was beginning to shoot forth fresh, spring-like growth. A new day was dawning. The earth had finally come up with an answer to the problems of disease, hunger, law breaking, and all sorts of the injustices of life. Life for man was getting better and better.

Many people erroneously thought as life was getting better, man, surely was getting better. In fact, a whole new system of theological dogma was being formed. Some argued that since everything was getting better and man was getting better, we were to usher in the great Millennium so long predicted by the prophets. Block by block, theorem by theorem, all this was built into what I prefer to call the "American Dream." I realize what I am here describing is only a part of the broad classification of the American Dream, but none-the-less, our founding fathers were obsessed with the idea that the masses should be educated. Written into many laws of new states was the ordinance that one section of every township would be specifically appropriated and appointed to the public school. Probably you have given most of your local tax dollars to the care and maintenance of the school district in which you live. Not only local, but in many states up to two-thirds of state money goes into public education. The United States has committed itself to the education of the masses. A noble concept, but perhaps over the long haul one wonders, under its present management, can it be implemented fully for any duration of time?

Global civil wars and two great World Wars in the 20th century shattered the utopia sought by many of the 19th century scholars. The dream of education being the basis of world peace and coming utopia has died along with its founders and the millions of men who lie dead on battlefields of the Argonne Forest, Normandy, Guadalcanal, Hue, Beirut, and Jerusalem.

I do not plan to underestimate true education in this treatise, but I plan to subjugate my high school education to the light of objective criticism and dash it with humor along the way. In my own experience during the years 1952-56, I hoped this time would never end. It was a time of pure joy to me! During those years that I attended the American Public High School, three great things happened to me. I have arranged them below in ascending order. (Please hold your applause until all are introduced).

1. The knowledge of the arts and sciences I received was voluminous.
2. The knowledge I received about society and the social extra-curricular life was magnificent.
3. I found the elusive joy and purpose of life.

XVI

Cogito Ergo Sum

But I hungered and thirsted not after those first works of thine,
but after thee, thyself; THE TRUTH.
Augustine

How often have we all said, "There goes an educated person," or
"He is certainly well educated?" On these occasions, I casually ask
myself, "How do I know if a person is well educated?" By what criteria
do we judge education? How can we compare an Eaton graduate with
one from a high school in the Midwest? One answer might be the
person's performance on standardized tests given to a wide range of
random graduates, but then how do we measure the ability of the test
to measure what we want to measure? There, we are back round robin
to what we want to measure.

One might say, let's measure education by success in life.
Proceeding with the argument, what definition have we placed upon
success—the amount of money a person has amassed? Is financial
accruement a measure of success? To some, yes, but the vast majority
would not agree.

Can we say the number of books written or offices held by a person
is an indication of success? Or can we say that amassing a great store of
knowledge without any applicable use is education? Or working with
people and things diplomatically and with wisdom is where education
is?

I would propose that none of these taken individually, but all taken
collectively is really the basis for a person being well-educated.

In my frame of reference, I would say a definition of a good education would have to include the following but not preclude others added to this list. This list is a minimum, a must, if you will.

1. A working knowledge of Latin and/or Greek
2. Familiarity with a language other than the mother tongue, and not Latin or Greek
3. Ability to communicate in the mother tongue orally and verbally
4. A working knowledge of Chemistry, Mathematics and Physics (college level)
5. A college level introduction to ancient civilizations and the greater archeological field
6. A thorough knowledge of Christian Dogma and Western Christian Thought
7. A working knowledge of Western History and Thought
8. A simple knowledge of architectural procedures and tool use, with a familiarity of building materials
9. A college level knowledge of Biology and natural occurrences in Geology
10. A recognition of the Art masters and their greatest works
11. A recognition of the classics in Music and Literature
12. A practicing memorization of the rules of etiquette and decorum. (This might be called good taste.)
13. A college level acquaintance with the processes of the mind and abnormal thought
14. A wide social experience of group and individual contacts. This includes a wide travel and recreation schedule.
15. A speaking knowledge of stable trends in Literature, Music, Television, Radio and Theater. I here define stable as that condition of semi-permanence that has established the work as at least a standard in its medium. Semi-permanence must be at least five years.

I have met very few people I have considered well educated. In almost twenty years of teaching, I have met two that could converse at any level of this list. (Please do not think that I wrote the list from my own experience, because I consider myself to be pitifully weak on numbers 2, 9, and 15; however, I would like to think that I am striving to improve in even those weak areas.) I have always felt embarrassed when I chanced upon a conversation or fact that someone else knew and I didn't. This has always spurred my search to know and delve deeper into the truth of that subject. The sad part about the attitude of most people is they enjoy their ignorance and think it is a mark of accomplishment. It is no sin to be ignorant; the sin is in staying ignorant.

I personally have much more feeling of compassion for a person who has not had the chance of mental improvement, and is therefore, ignorant. Him I can help and he may progress farther than me, but the person with whom I have no truck is the one who has lived within walking distance of a library, school, or church and yet prefers to stay ignorant. Sad, but most of our contemporary society seems to love and admire the state of being ignorant.

XVII

The American High School: Circa 1955

But the tender grace of a day that is dead will never come back to me.
Tennyson

Some five years ago, a remark was made by one of the upper echelon leaders of our nation. I quote that remark. "The young people today are better educated and have more knowledge and are better at problem solving than any of all history. They have more wisdom and knowledge than we ever had."

Well, I certainly cannot speak for that person, but if that were true, then I would offer him a guide dog to get around from place to place. He certainly was not speaking for me or my high school or college group.

To this famous man's statement I would respond, "bullfeathers." This statement reflects the general "Worship of Youth Cult" which ran rampant during the 60's and 70's—a cult one certainly hopes has abated some during the second half of the seventies. To have this cult continue would certainly mean a quick demise to our present way of life. Youth has neither the maturity nor the strength of moral fiber to withstand the rigors of adult leadership and daily decisions. Young people, at their best, are undependable and weak-willed.

This leader's statement, so incredulous and irresponsible, started me thinking about the American High School and the youth culture through which I passed on the road to education and hopefully, maturity.

*   *   *

September 1952, not quite fourteen years of age, I stood petrified on the steps of the giant multi-columned edifice called Thomas Jefferson School, situated imposingly on the main street of Belaire.

Every so often one has an experience he thinks should never end. He revels in the pure ecstasy of it and once ended, he savors it over and over until the grim reaper takes the pilgrim home. Such an experience was the few years I spent at that tower of intellectual worship. The time spent there was every moment a pleasure, every day a new treat, academically and socially.

At that time, Jefferson High School had all the ingredients of not just a good school, but an excellent one. It had tradition on its side. Far and away, Jefferson rated the best school in the city, and perhaps the best in the state at that time.

Socio-economically, most parents of students were high middle class and upper class. This does not necessarily make for a good education, but it does show these parents had the means to give their children a wider experience in most of the fifteen areas of education mentioned previously. Many of the Jefferson graduates were already through college and making their mark of leadership in the community and the nation. There were several in business and on the school board.

The school already had built a case for scholarship. The work was not easy and some failed. Students did not pass simply because it would hurt their psyche to fail. Easy passing leads to dropping the standards of excellence. Goal-oriented people see no need of the soft labor. For most of these types of people, the struggle is the goal.

It was difficult. I worked hard while I was there. Many of my classmates and I wrote research papers in high school that upper division college students would be hard pressed to duplicate. I look back on the courses we simply called English I, II, III . . . . VIII and marvel at the things I did. We spent five days a week in grammar, straight grammar, the first year. Although years of sloppy writing have taken their toil, I still remember many of the basics learned there. (The other part of my writing, I now classify under the broad category of poetic license.) As we progressed, we spent the tenth grade in three days of grammar. Finally, I tested into five days of literature my senior year.

This senior year of literature was like a little bit of heaven. The days spent in reading during elementary and junior high school now gave me a vent to a scholarly approach to literature in high school.

We read and analyzed all of Shakespeare's plays and fifty of his better-known sonnets. I devoured Homer, Ovid, Virgil, Eusebius, Eschyulus, Euripides, Caesar, Cicero, Josephus, Heroditus, Aurileus, Augustine, Jerome . . . ah, the joy goes on and on.

I chose for my senior project in literature, "The Song of Roland." I went through all of the material in our school library and spent several nights at the public library downtown. This report consisted of a one half hour oral report to the class and a twenty (or more) written report then placed on file in the school library. Shoddy work was unacceptable. Excellence was just barely good enough. To top it off, all of this work was to be done outside of class.

During class, we dissected Milton and Dante and watched poor Beatrice on her lonely journey. Such authors as Johnson, Bacon, Byron, Pope, Pepys, Shelley, Wordsworth, Keats, and Yeats were on our lighter reading schedule. Browning, (there I felt was true greatness), was a must for me. He moved me perhaps as no other author could. To this day, I read and re-read his "Rabii Ben Esra" with tears in my eyes, Of course, there is his "Incident at a French Camp" which I encountered in elementary school with Bill. The native returned with Hardy, I fought the great white with Melville, killed the king's men with Dumas, and on they came in an endless stream. I traveled the globe with these great men. Now in Paris, then on the high seas, London, India, in the south sea. I could pass from the 20th century to the 14th or 16th or any century I wanted just by turning the page.

I went through the first two books of Chaucer in the old English translation as I went. I discovered that the translation was not worth the effort for it was very dull to me. Surprisingly, this classic piece was one of the few that really shut off my mind. I personally thought the work was written poorly and in bad taste, but most of all dull, Dull, DULL! I did enjoy the first twenty or so lines of the prologue, where he describes the springtime walk of the pilgrims. The rest is hardly worth the trip, even in English.

I spent the junior year of English with short stories and essays. The mixture of humor and deeper philosophical works was excellent and kept the edge of my excitement. I started with the simpler humorous essays of Benchley and Leacock then switched to John Stuart Mill, Bertrand Russell, and labored over the Huxley Boys. True, at this time, I did not fully appreciate the deeper meanings of Benthem, Hume, Kant, and Butler. At this point, I had not enough experience to understand their implied meanings. I reread them again in college and they made considerable more sense even though I disagreed violently with some of them, especially Kant, Mill, and Nietzsche.

It was during these tenth and eleventh years of school, I met two teachers who so beautifully completed the job that Beverly Martin had started in the fifth and sixth grades. Bonnie Jean O'Rourke and Sally Markam were to finish the job of turning me on to great literature. I shall forever be in their debt. After they were finished with me, I was hopelessly trapped in the web of vicarious excitement that they had woven about me. I could do nothing else but wallow in the trough of great literature.

I have struggled long and laboriously to unravel the motivating force that these two women held and used on me in hopes that I too might use it, but alas, I am still as puzzled as the day I left them, never to see them these twenty years. Yet I see them both clearly in my mind, the complete antithesis of each other.

Bonnie Jean O'Rourke was young, pretty and vivacious. She was a prime marriageable target. In our senior year, I think some rumor was about she was going to be wed soon after our departure from the hallowed halls of ivy. I even remember clearly the room where we met. Each morning I would rush into the room second period, prepared for mental gymnastics with "Miss O'Rourke'". She was a tall girl with a pointed chin and high cheekbones. Straight white teeth lay behind rather thin lips and a large sensual mouth. Narrow eyes broke the high forehead just right while long black hair lay in rolls covering both ears from view. She was slim enough so that the cords of her neck and clavicle protruded especially when she was chastising us. Her figure was pleasing to the male eye, lithe and supple. I only remember one flaw in her presentation—her thighs and ankles were rather stocky in nature. She had the rich Irish fire so characteristic of the fabled isle. Those eyes could snap and throw flame clear across the room. She was an energetic sort, one who accomplished large volumes of work easily. I suppose this was part of my identification with her. She was only slightly moody, as I did not have trouble knowing this bit of melancholia.

About Christmas time 1953, the bell had already rung and Miss O'Rourke was giving us instructions concerning the writing of descriptive narrative when suddenly there was an obviously dissonant knock on the classroom door. Noticeably perturbed at the interruption, she walked swiftly to the door and opened it to reveal a tall, mature man about 28 years of age. Without saying a word, he swept her up into his arms, swung her back into a dip, planted a rough kiss squarely on her lips and held it for perhaps 30 seconds. He then set her once again on her feet, smiled, left the room and closed the door behind him. Not a word did he speak. We were all aghast!!! She, primping her hair and straightening her blouse and skirt said to us, "Now write. Describe what you just saw." Motivation is not the proper word. I wrote like my pencil was alive.

Sally Markam, on the other hand, was as different from Miss O'Rourke as day and night. The only thing they had in common was the fact that I loved their classes enormously. Their classes were not only intellectually stimulating, but they were fun—good old-fashioned fun.

Miss Markam was a slightly built lady in her fifties. She was the prototype of the schoolteacher. She was proper, staid, extremely kind, well respected, and loved by those that passed through her classes. Her dress and decorum was conservative, expensive, in good taste and above reproach. Her clothes were loose enough to be unrevealing yet tight enough not to be sloppy. She had a kindly face and wore wire-rimmed glasses, worn for necessity rather than fad, like today sometimes. She was graceful, cultured and well read. I always thought she knew most anything about everything, unlike some of her contemporaries under whom I sat at Jefferson High School.

* * *

I did have two teachers I would describe best as dolts or culls. These two were dull, witless and totally unmotivating, but will only share further about one of these people. I felt the two semesters I spent in their classes was a waste of my time and the taxpayers money. Incidentally, my brother lost all love of reading under the tutelage of one of them. He came home continually depressed and regressed until he finally gave up. A decision, which made sooner, might have saved his reading desire. Now he seldom reads for pleasure, only for necessity.

In my own situation, I merely considered these classes a nuisance, a cross to bear for eighteen weeks. Having borne the cross, I slipped back into the old excitement of reading again. I wish I were in the classes of Markam or O'Rourke for those two semesters. I could have had 36 weeks more of the pleasure of discovery, of excitement, of wit and humor. Unfortunately, there are times when all of us, as Milton put it, just stand and wait. These two semesters were of that genre.

During those two witless semesters, other things took over my mind to take up the slack. I spent most of the time in class with pranks and jokes so characteristic of the adolescent mind. I shall not soon forget the day that Mr. Bummer placed each one of us in separate corners of the room. Bill was back in the right rear corner of the room near the large windows. On this gigantic window hung a huge shade that covered the entire block of windows. I suppose the shade was about 10 feet wide and ran the full length of the window. When unrolled, it was a distance of about 12 feet. Bill proceeded to open the window to give the class the benefit of the fresh spring air.

Mr. Bummer called out from the front of the room, "Mr. Rogers, are you authorized to ventilate the room?"

"No Sir." Bill said.

Whereupon, Mr. Bummer strode confidently to the rear of the room and rather sharply closed the window. He then gave the shade a quick yank to let it go to the top. When he did this, the entire shade came off the wall and the wood roller hit him on the head knocking him to the floor. The shade unrolled over him like a shroud over a dead man. He was lying on the floor in the room yelling and kicking like a kid under a blanket. A foot, then an arm came through the shade while their owner kept calling for us to help him.

Bill made the following remark, "We're not authorized to help you."

This only added fuel to the already tender situation. I certainly did not forget this little escapade quickly.

Mr. Bummer also had a couple of bad habits that became part of our regular sport. I have concluded that the whole thing must have been as boring to him as to us. The class was punctuating sentences orally when Mr. Bummer called on Marie to read the sentence and punctuate it. Marie responded by reading the sentence and punctuating it correctly. Mr. Bummer then said, "Now punctuate it please." From the back of the room (Bill) came a low, guttural voice that said, "Use Bell-Tone hearing aids." All of us just fell out of our chairs. Bill was kicked out for three days.

* * *

The days I spent with Caesar and Cicero in Latin were just as rewarding as those in English. Unlike many, I easily grasped Latin and it was a veritable joy. After four years of Latin, I got to the place where I could write and translate almost as fluently as English. I cannot say enough for the care and study of the Latin language. Except for Greek, Latin is the basic language of English and the other civilized languages. Latin and Greek are not only the cornerstones of our language, but also the cradle of civilization. They, with Hebrew, hold the basic keys to all known knowledge, the written history of man on this planet, and the access route to God himself.

In no other languages can one discipline himself so much, learn so much grammar, increase his English vocabulary, become so knowledgeable as to why we are like we are, and understand so many jokes and puns as he can with the knowledge of these two languages. The four years I spent with this language formally were some of my best intellectually, even if I did not know it fully at the time.

Latin gave me a chance to ride with Caesar into Gaul, to sit with Cicero in the Senate, and to ply my strength on the good ship Argos. It was a time of discovering Olympus and its treasures of mythical hanky-panky. General rules of decency and morality did not bother the gods and heroes of the Romans and Greeks. In fact, they so represented the attitudes of those degenerated civilizations in their final stages of decay.

The last year final in Latin was a wonder to behold. I was to make an after school appointment with the instructor, an immense lady of gigantic proportions but not altogether fat. I was to, in her words, "Come and be prepared to read Latin."

The fateful appointment came and I knocked softly on the door of her office. She answered the door, smiled and nodded toward the chair at her desk. She sat down in the large green leather office chair, crossed her immense legs and looked at the clock. She turned slightly and took two identical books from her bookcase. I strained my eyes and just caught part of the title. I was relieved. It was Augustine. It was too much to hope that it might be his *City of God* or *Confessions* because I had read both of them in English and was somewhat familiar with the flow of the language. She handed me one of the books and said, "Don't open it until I tell you to do so." I grasped the book eagerly and got the full title. What luck! It was Augustine alright, *Confessions*.

I now entertained thoughts that I might even pass this examination. I had none before.

The object of the examination was that she would tell me to start reading in English from the Latin text at a random point of her selection. I had to read 1000 lines in a specified period of time with a predetermined minimum of mistakes—a tough order by any stretch of the imagination.

After several lines, I began to relax and get into the actual thought of what Augustine was saying rather than just translating words. I began to see the sentences in thoughts rather than individual words. I began to enjoy the thoughts and partially put my large Latin mentor out of my mind, as if I were reading in my room stretched out over my bed.

The time passed quickly when finally this voice from somewhere out there said, "Okay that's far enough." Then we sat and talked about Latin, the school and my home for about 20 minutes. I left knowing that graduation now loomed as a distinct possibility in my future.

I feel I had a distinct advantage my first year of college due to the knowledge thus obtained and the instructors I met during high school. I worked hard at four years of Latin, English, History and Government, Mathematics, two years of Chemistry, Physics, Biology and several electives. This was tough work, but despite the rigors of academia, I think I managed one of the better social lives as well.

XVIII

Boola–Boola, Boola–Boola . . . Etc.

By many waters and on many ways
I have known golden instants and bright days.
John Masefield

The pleasurable experience of high school lasted for several years. The time flew by with alacrity and I savored each experience to taste again and again, draining every drop of pleasure from the erstwhile moment. Such was the description of the adolescent social life of my academic thoroughfare.

It is difficult to know what exactly to call up from this time as evidence of my search for life's purpose. This period was full of so many hedonistic experiences that were not immoral necessarily in the traditional sense of the word, but none-the-less sensual.

The dynamics of an adolescent group are always interesting to observe especially if one is not particularly associated as a functioning part of the group. It has been my good fortune to observe many such groups in this capacity. Because of this observation, I can now look back on my experiences with a critical, objective eye. The social organization of the group with which I was associated was circular in nature with widening circles about the particular group, illustrated below.

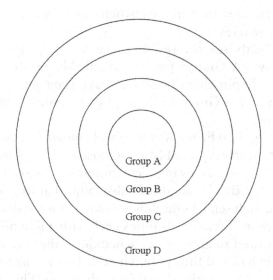

Group A is composed of two to eight members—very rarely more than eight members and usually of the same sex. Group B is composed of twenty to fifty members. Usually it contains three to ten Group As (depending on the size of the Group As). It also depends on common morality standards. Group C contains three to ten Group Bs, and Group D usually contains an entire school.

One will notice that the morality standard of the group ("Rules" to be accepted in the group) mentioned earlier changes radically as the group circles widen.

Thus, it is very easy to fit into and be a part of a Group D, but one must adhere to relatively rigid standards to be a member of an A Group, particularly in a leadership capacity. This is the obvious reason for all schools having a group of hoods or degenerates. They do not have the moral fiber to be members of a respectable A Group. Thus, several form their own A group with their obvious degenerate standards. It has been my observation that this group can be capable of almost anything once the stamp of approval has been put on it by the entire group. A member of this group can and often does function entirely different as a part of the group than while speaking or talking to others outside of the group, especially adults.

I would say the real mental crisis of an adolescent comes when he finds that for one reason or another, he cannot be part of any Groups, A through D. This child is the one who is likely dangerous to himself and others. When several of these meet and form a substandard A Group (meaning that their A Group cannot be members of B, C or D) then the problems are immense and overwhelming to home, school and law enforcement agencies.

One can clearly see the problem is in identifying the difference between the two A Groups just described. Maybe the difference is only academic. I split them because I have seen some emerge from the first described A Group to be solid conscientious citizens, never from the second.

The A Group in which I was involved contained seven members: three liberal Protestants (possibly non-Christians), two Jews, one Greek Orthodox, and myself, an evangelical Protestant. Characteristic of this group was the fact that it contained sub-groups that were continuously changing. The high school schedule was such that the day was divided into seven periods, fifty-five minutes each with a five minute passing time. I always tried to arrange my schedule so that the fourth period would be study hall and fifth period lunch. This arrangement meant I was free from 11:20am until 1:20pm for sixth period. This two hour time block held a myriad of wonders for the perceptive pleasure seeker. At the end of third period, each one of our group would run to the parking lot and speed out to Roco's Drive In on Ryan Road. We would spend the time eating and setting up the evenings social arrangements.

One day as we were hustling back from Roco's, Bill was driving and we were late. The car was rolling down Sheean across Adams at about 1:20pm. The bell had already rung as we pulled onto Main Street in front of the school. All of the occupants of the car jumped out and started to run for typing class on the second floor in the back, leaving Bill to park the car and make it to class. I was running as hard as I could when I looked over my shoulder and saw Bill not more than thirty feet behind the pack. I yelled back and asked Bill where he had found a parking space so quickly. Bill breathlessly stated that he didn't. I then took a fleeting glimpse back at Main and noticed Bill's car was perched motionless in the middle of the busy thoroughfare where Bill had abandoned it. Traffic was already backing up in both directions. Up the back stairs and chugging down the hall, Bill lost a little more off the pace. I made it into the room just as Bill was turning the corner from the stairs into the hall.

Mr. Bendix was talking to another student. He had one hand on the doorknob of the multi-paned Eisen glass door. As the bell started to ring, I saw Bill about 10 feet from the door. Mr. Bendix pulled the door shut when the bell rang. The next scene is pathetic to describe. Bill came crashing through the glass door and splintered the small wood moldings. As the bell finished its ring, Bill hung half in the room through the broken door, blood dripping from his arms and head.

He looked up and said to Mr. Bendix, "Are you going to count me late?"

That evening was spent at the police impound yard freeing Bill's car!!!

XIX

Smoking May Be Hazardous to Your Health

But hollow men, like horses hot at hand,
Make gallant show and promise of their mettle;
But when they should endure the bloody spur,
They fall their crests, and, like deceitful jades,
Sink in the trial.
Shakespeare

The scene: January 1955, Friday night after a basketball game with John Adams High School, four degrees below zero. Our group was in Chick's (sometimes called Chickie or Chickweed) '54 two-tone brown Mercury driving across town. Chick wheeled off Hill Street west onto Washington. We abruptly stopped at the drugstore on the corner of Washington and Main. John piled out of the car and went into the apothecary shop. Emerging a few minutes later, he carried a carton of king size filter cigarettes.

No one opened the package until we pulled into our familiar parking space at Roco's. The intense cold had fogged over all the windows and the engine was running for the heater's warmth. John gave each a full pack, and we all opened it and drew one to each of our lips. None of us had yet tried the wily art. We all lit up simultaneously. The smoke began to be suffocating as we puffed ceremoniously. In fact, the smoke was so thick that it was difficult to see the others in

---

the car. The air was blue with smoke as we changed from cigarettes to several cigars John found in the glove compartment.

Twenty minutes later, we all sat quietly stupefied and glassy-eyed. Suddenly, I could take it not a minute longer. I burst out of the right rear of the car and fell to the cold curb outside vomiting like a sick hog. Dry heaves took over as dinner and lunch vacated the premises. I lay on the cold concrete until the frozen chill caught up with my inebriated brain.

Inadvertently, this turned out to be one of the best things that happened to me. Since that frozen day in 1955, I have never touched that noxious weed. To this day in restaurants or planes, I go into an asthmatic seizure when the impish weed is burning within ten feet of me. I have yet to figure out if the aversion attacks are remembering that night in my youth or an actual allergic reaction.

XX

A Little Knowledge is a Dangerous Thing
or The Care and Feeding of a Dar

"A Dar," you ask, "What is a Dar?"

There happened to be among my mentors, a male instructor of chemistry whose initials (which he wrote so generously on passes and important papers) spelled the word "Dar". Each of us had grown to love this balding foundation of our school. Dar was a tall man in safety glasses and a rubber apron. His mind was bright and his outlook was young despite his approaching retirement years. It was my good fortune to learn volumes from the mind that was under his polished hoary fringed dome, sometimes more than I should or even cared to know.

Case in point.

Several of my peers and I walked into the room one day expecting a rather routine lab demonstration. I, along with the rest, were strewn aimlessly (in typical teenage fashion) about the lab table expecting the Great Dar to appear and tantalize us with his bits of chemical trickery. Dar strode into the room carrying an evaporating dish with what looked like a pea or soy bean in a liquid resting carefully in the bottom. The class was mildly quizzical.

Dar informed us that this was a small piece of Potassium. He went to the board and wrote:

$$2K+2HOH=2KOH+H_2$$

Then he went back to the table, picked up the Potassium with forceps and dropped it into a beaker of water. The reaction was instantaneous and spectacular! The heat of this reaction ignites the escaping Hydrogen and the water literally decomposes and burns. This made a profound impression on each one of us about the table. I suppose we all were thinking of the same possibilities.

That evening Chickweed picked me up and we headed straight to Roco's Drive-in. We met the remainder of our group and started formulating the execution of our plan. The father of a friend of ours was the owner of a large pharmaceutical house. Therefore, we needed to enlist this friend in the plan. We all piled into Chick's car and drove over to Jerry's house. Informed of the escapade, Jerry got into the car and we drove to his father's business establishment. Chick pulled the car over and parked it about two blocks from the watchman's gate. Jerry and I walked along the sidewalk to the watchman's gate. Jerry was immediately recognized by the watchman and both of us were passed through. Using his father's keys, we walked up the back stairs to the main warehouse. Jerry flipped on the lights and I started looking. We were in the chemical warehouse and fortunately, everything was arranged in alphabetical order. All of a sudden there it was—a large box with a gigantic K (potassium) on the label. I was home free. I opened the box and inside was a rather large glass jar with a potassium brick submerged in Kerosene. The brick was about 2½ inches wide, 5 inches long and 2 inches thick. Jerry picked up an empty box, partially filled it with sawdust, put the potassium bottle inside, and covered it over with sawdust. I sealed the empty K box shut and put it back on the shelf behind two full ones. Down the stairs, past the guard and into the car we went. Chick revved up the car and we sped away to Roco's, rollicking and laughing all the way.

I must admit in the back of my mind, I visualized police cars swarming around our car and being led away in handcuffs, but as life would have it, most of the things we worry about never happen. Conversely, most of our major problems come as bolts from out of the blue-things about which we have never thought or even dared to think. Further, most of the problems we do face never really turn out to be nearly as bad as we had originally supposed. This is perhaps the reason why one should never make major decisions between the hours of 11pm and 5:30am. These are times when the darkness seems to envelope one's thoughts, but with the morning comes hope and a clearer picture of the night's problems.

The night's problems were running through my mind as we cruised along the river on the Ryan Road toward the footbridge across the river. The car pulled up short into the little walkway to the footbridge. I jumped out with the rest of the group. Chickweed carried the precious package onto the bridge, and we all followed wild-eyed and scared. I stood and watched Chickie unscrew the wide-mouthed top of the jar. Not a word was spoken as he cautiously lifted the jar to the top of the guardrail. We waited with bated breath for the exciting moment to arrive. My mouth was dry and I felt like I was chewing on my tongue. I noticed my eyes were watery as I saw the jar turned upside down. All of us simultaneously rushed to the guardrail to watch the first happenings. The brick hit the water and THE SHOW WAS ON!

Looking back, none of us expected the brilliant display of fireworks that ensued. It was beautiful; the whole river was engulfed in flames in just a few minutes. I thought for a while the wooden footbridge was going to go. We ran like crazy to the car, and Chick threw it into gear and tore away back to Roco's. Upon arriving, we saw the crowd already gathering as they had spotted the massive display about a mile upriver. The river flowed toward Roco's and town, so this brought the fire closer and closer toward the gathering group.

I was beginning to feel the impact of the whole enterprise. I was so hoping that the last reaction would soon burn itself out. It didn't. I watched horrified as sirens blared in my ears. Fire trucks, hook and ladders, and squad cars swarmed the entire area.

I have long since wondered what the fireman thought as he took that first fire call. I imagine when he heard the voice on the other end of the line say, "I would like to report that the river is on fire," he certainly would have some terse comment for the obvious prankster or drunk.

As all normal teenagers, I spent the rest of the evening with my cronies "crowing" about the greatness of the event and the masterful way we had handled the entire affair.

I watched the last firetruck load up its gear, the police disbanding the crowd, and Roco's beginning to empty toward closing. I wandered about the drive-in for a few minutes with mixed emotions. On the one hand, I felt like the land baron going about visiting his serfs and receiving their congratulations for the nice way his visit was affecting their lives. I was William the Conqueror, Charlemagne, and Caesar all rolled into one, and I was riding the crest of the wave.

Hours later, as I lay in my bed going over the events of the day, the wave crested and broke over such a feeling of depression that it is difficult to describe. That old nagging feeling was back after the thrill had subsided, back to haunt me again. Once again, I began to think there is something else. There is surely more to life than that moment of passing ecstasy, then total and complete gloom and dismalness.

I could then feel the hot breath of God on my neck as He was gaining on me and I was tiring of the pace.

SOMETHING HAD BETTER HAPPEN SOON.

XXI

Labora Omnes Est

Perhaps my semblance might deceive the truth,
That I to manhood am arriv'd so near . . .
John Milton

My parents and I decided I had too much free time, so the following week I made an appointment to see Bill Warden, Dean of Men, about a job he had posted on the school bulletin board. He gave me the information, and I stopped that evening after school to see Jim Michaels, owner and operator of Michael's Gourmet Shop.

Mr. Michaels was a man in his late 50's with grown children. His son and daughter were both graduates of Jefferson, and I suppose this is the reason he wanted another Jefferson kid to work for him. Jim was almost blind and couldn't drive. My job was to do all the delivery work, keep the books, and drive him around. The job started this way, but towards the end, it evolved into being general manager of the entire operation. Later, he even offered the entire business to me, but I declined, as I wanted to finish college.

The business consisted of gourmet foods I delivered every Friday evening and Saturday. During the week, Jim would be on the phone selling items. On Friday, he would give me the orders and where I should deliver them. I would then get all the orders ready and enter names and amounts in the books on Friday night. Then on Saturday I loaded and delivered all materials to their desired owners.

The clientele was the upper class because the foods that he handled were very expensive. Items such as pears, peaches, and other fruits packed in brandy, smoked herring, lox and caviar, sausages, hams, special and exotic fruits were on the menu. Unique blends of tea and coffee were the specialties of the house.

Jim always had experimental tea and coffee around. I developed a taste for good tea during this time—A taste that has haunted my taste buds as I hopelessly roam the aisles of our large present day supermarkets. As for coffee, most of the coffee he sold was heavy on chicory, a flavor I have never been able to tolerate. To this day, I feel coffee is the scourge of our civilization and a bane to urbane living.

Several years ago, one of my very best friends, a physician, and I were talking. He asked me why I did not care for coffee. This is what I told him. During my junior year of college, I had four cups of coffee one evening. The next day I had an attack of appendicitis and was hospitalized with an appendectomy. Never, since that night, have I had a cup of coffee because I considered the coffee brought on my appendicitis. He asked me how I knew it was the coffee. I replied, "Well, it hasn't happened again since I quit!"

I recall two of my favorite places to deliver, a large seventy-two room mansion of a rather large local business owner and the nunnery of the Roman Catholic Cathedral. I got lost in the basement of the mansion the first time I delivered there. The butler took me down the stairs and the hallway opened into a large game room that contained four pool tables, two billiard tables, two ping-pong tables, five pin ball machines, and several other arcade items. Also, the basement had a five lane bowling alley, an archery range, a large walk-in freezer and refrigerator, a storm or bomb shelter, a gigantic food storage pantry, a large swimming pool, a lounge and bar. I moved from room to room trying to find the stairs, but I must admit I was curious as to what all was down there. The owner had a son about my age I had met a couple of summer's earlier at Hopewell Golf Club. When I delivered there, I would usually spend some time taking him at pool or bowling. Sometimes when he was gone, I would play the pinball machines or bowl a couple of frames by myself. They had a maid who was a real whiz at pool. She could sometimes run two racks without missing. It was a real treat to run half a rack with her, and she taught me a lot about Geometry.

The other place I found quite pleasurable was the nun's quarters at the Cathedral. Several Saturday mornings found me sitting around the kitchen table talking religion, politics or basketball with those hooded ladies of the church. Most of them were, I felt, born-again Christians. Of course, there were some who seemed bogged down in the traditionalism of liturgy and didn't have the time or inclination to know in a personal way the living Christ, but most of the ladies were kind, thoughtful Christian ladies who in word and deed were in their daily lives showing forth the love of Christ. True, they were tied and constrained by the forms and rituals of the church to the point where it was somewhat difficult to live the Christian life in its oppressive and often nonbiblical practices, but once stripping all the trappings away and getting through the jargon of thought and traditional dogma, there were many followers of Christ there. I enjoyed talking and discussing with them immensely for several reasons.

1. They knew Latin and were well versed in classical literature.
2. They knew the Scriptures and knew what they meant.
3. They were well educated and intelligent.
4. They knew what was going on in the world outside their cloisters.

In fact, given the proper circumstances, a lot could be said for their particular way of life. I was impressed by their education and single purpose, but not too impressed with the evolution of their theology. One of my favorite topics was asking them if they still followed the teachings of Aquinas and Augustine. When they obviously said yes, I would start to ask them about certain items where, in my judgment, the church has moved away from their teachings. This prompted much conversation and heated discussion. After a time, I would have to continue my rounds. I would bid the ladies in black farewell, and go on to the next customer.

The pay was certainly good on this job. Sometimes during one weekend, I could make $100 to $180. Jim gave me 10% of everything that came through the store, and on a poor week we would run about $500. The best week I remember was about $2700. The only overhead I had was gasoline and depreciation on my car. Since my father took care of the car, I only had to buy the gasoline. At this time I had a '51 Plymouth Belvedere that got about 20 miles to the gallon. Gas was only running at 26¢ per gallon. I had quite a bit left from my work at Michaels.

XXII

Flash: High School Youth Digs to China

Fame is no plant that grows on mortal soil.
John Milton

The birds had all returned to the north. The buds were pushing out the ends of the brown twigs and the soft warm zephyrs were wafting in the tall half-open windows. The minds inside the room were on sunny days at the beach, baseball games in the park and all the other sunshine activities of summer.

All students (and teachers) were counting the school days of spring like a prisoner marking the days off on the wall of his cell. These lazy days of spring had a stifling effect on my mind. I have never really appreciated the spring season for this very reason. It always seemed to me spring was a time for an end, not the beginning so fabled by the poets. The soft, warm, lazy days were suffocating to my mind and made my body feel like not moving for days.

This season always signaled the end of school and rang a note of sadness as the scene changed. The full schedule of activities changed to the slowness and sadness of *Pomp and Circumstance*. This musical work brought the old stab of purpose, joy and fulfillment to me in a slightly different way then crashing Joey's crater or discussing with the nun, but still the same stab, still the same feeling that mixes contentment with depression and hopelessness. I couldn't explain that feeling but it always came on the heels of the thrill or joy of some temporal pleasure. That same feeling always asked the same haunting question, "Isn't there more to it all? Is this it? Is this all there is to it? There has got to be more."

During the graduation season, there was a rite of spring at Jefferson called Ivy Day. This was the time when the entire school became embroiled in the traditions of the academic community. The day was spent in electing the Ivy Queen and her court, bestowing of academic awards, the Ivy Day program, and last, but certainly not least, was the planting of the ivy. The school was almost completely covered by the overgrown plantings of past Ivy Days. Each year for the past 35 years, the single sprig of ivy had grown to gargantuan proportions.

Ivy Day was also the opening of the graduation season and closing of school activities. Bill and I were seated in the junior section of the honors program. Mr. B. was just beginning the typing awards. I knew I was in for a long, boring session as the typing awards were always astronomical in number and inconsequential in worth. Mr. B. had just finished the Best-Typist-with-the-Small-Finger-on-the-Left-Hand in the 35-Word-Per-Minute-9½-Mistakes-on-a-Manual-1937-Typewriter category, when suddenly Miss Grant came down the aisle to where we were sitting. We thought for a minute we might be in big trouble.

A comment about this feeling might be in order here. I knew, as many youths know, that while I was sitting there, I had nothing to fear because currently, I was doing nothing of an illegal nature. But the fear of being in big trouble came to me after I rehearsed in my mind the number of things for which I could be harshly chastised from my past. Thus, the feeling of fear that I could be in big trouble is justified because guilt brings all the obstreperous actions to mind again and again and again.

This fact bothered me many thousands of times since my "conversion" in 1949, but I was powerless to control the feelings of guilt until a day almost a year later from this point in the narrative.

Miss Grant stopped by our chairs and stooped over to whisper something to us. "Each year," she said, "We choose two people to plant the ivy and this year we have chosen you and Bill. Now, come with me and we will make the preparations for the Ivy ceremonies."

We both stood and left with her. She took us down the back stairs and into the gardener's room on the back northeast corner of the school. She told us to get a couple of shovels and a garden trowel and meet her at the northwest corner of the school, where the ivy was to be planted.

Bill and I reconnoitered through the rummage (We both were great trash hunters.) to see what was there. After several minutes of nosing around, we picked up a pair of long-handled shovels, a small trowel and slowly ambled toward the appointed spot.

I heard Mr. B on the PA system. He was now down to Best-9-Fingered-Male-Typist-in-a-Blue-Shirt-on-Tuesday/Friday-Electric category. I was so glad to move away from the speaker and not be forced to listen to that drivel for two and half hours.

Miss Grant met us and pointed to the place where she wanted the ivy planted. She said for us to loosen the area with the big shovels and then leave a hole to plant the ivy later. When finished, we were to return to the honors program. She left. I noted that we now had a problem. The work she left for us to do would take us, at the most, five to six minutes. Mr. B was now down to Best-Typist-Absent-Only-on-the-Second-Thursday-of-the-Fourth-Week-of-the-Six-Weeks-Period-in-Third-Period-Electric-Keyboard-Manual-Carriage category. No way did I want to return to that.

So Bill and I started digging . . . slowly . . . trying to kill time. We dragged out the job as long as we dared. At this time, neither Bill nor I paid a whole lot of attention to what we were doing until I noticed that we were both about waist high in the hole. Both of us noticed the humor of the situation right away. Immediately, we started digging like crazy until the hole was about chest high. Miss Grant came back and found a pile of dirt and behind it a hole with two heads sticking out of it. Bill looked out of the hole and said, "We're ready for the ivy."

Miss Grant was mildly irritated until she saw the humor of planting that small sprig of ivy in that mammoth hole. She started laughing and only stopped long enough to tell us to get that hole filled in fifteen minutes.

That year in the Annual, a picture of a large hole with two heads appeared in the graduation section with the caption: FLASH: YOUTHS DIG TO CHINA.

XXIII

All Work and No Play Makes Jack a Dull Boy

Oh what fools we mortals be.
Shakespeare

In any institution, it always seems that the young, the naive, and the frail seem to receive more than their share of ribbing and flagging. In the halls of secondary school, it seems the freshmen take their licks from the seniors and others who know the ropes.

Each year during the first week of school, the school paper would print a copy of the entire floor plan of the school with accompanying room numbers, teacher's names, and general tidbits of information. This printing was invaluable to the new and the ignorant. The freshmen guarded those maps with their lives and depended on them, even if a misprint or incorrect information appeared.

One of the aspects of the geography of Jefferson H.S. was an oddity called "Girls Locker Rooms" and "Boys Locker Rooms". These were halls that were about sixty feet wide and ran the entire length of the Study Hall, which was 26 rows deep. The rooms were large enough to house the lockers of ¾ of the 2200 students attending the school. These two rooms lay on either side of a massive study hall. (See picture).

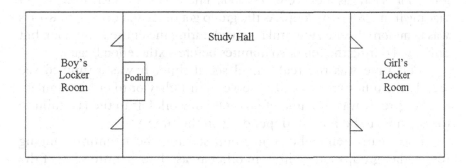

This study hall was twenty-six rows wide and twenty-six seats deep. A Gestapo agent in hiding since WWII operated it. Seriously, the proctor ran a very tight ship. I have seen her throw high school seniors twice her size against the wall in a daze. She sat on a high podium in the rear of the study hall. No one talked, moved or walked around the hall between bells.

Of course, the figure shown above was only a small part of the total complex. It was this complex that gave the freshmen fits during their first few weeks there.

As seniors, the sport of the first few weeks was mesmerizing the freshmen. These frail little people would walk from place to place with terror in their eyes and their maps clutched tightly in their hands. One of our favorite tricks was to stand in the large multi-lined locker room and watch a freshmen struggling with his lock. It was a quick and easy matter to memorize his combination while he was trying to open it. After his exit, one would simply step to his locker and unlock it. Several of us would be doing this at the same time. Next, we would switch two freshmen locks from opposite ends of the locker room and relocked. The sport came in watching the frosh come to his locker at the next passing time. He would work and work trying to unlock his locker. Being late to class was the next step and trouble with the authorities was imminent. Usually about two periods later, Mr. Warden would be down to the locker room followed by ten to twelve meek-mannered freshmen. In his hand was a master key and in his eye was disgust. The lock numbers were once again matched with the locker numbers, and all tried their locks to make sure the locks were back on the correct lockers.

Not quite as much fun but still rather exhilarating was the gathering of eagles in the gym during noon hour. Each C group would stake out a claim of area in the gym as freshmen. This would be the area of the group for as long as they were in school. There was very little mingling or visiting from group to group. As the group got older and driving to Roco's was common, the area was still reserved during the entire noon hour, but only used during the ten or so minutes before sixth period began.

This time was the real school social time. It was a time to see clearly the other groups and observe their behavior to either emulate or castigate. It was the time of doing homework left to the last minute (or copying, to be honest, depending on the time.)

I so clearly remember our group starting the noontime singing fest. Other groups joined in from other areas. The favorite song of the combined groups seems silly to recount. It was a children's song with very little meaning, quite different from the scholarly work the group had just left in class.

Oh little playmate come out and play with me,
And bring your dollies three,
Climb up my apple tree,
Shout down my rain barrel,
Slide down my cellar door,
And we'll be jolly friends forevermore.

But little playmate,
I cannot play with you,
My dollies have the flu,
Boo-hoo-hoo-hoo-hoo-hoo,
Ain't got no rain barrel,
Ain't got no cellar door,
But we'll be jolly friends forevermore.

These long years later, I taught this song to my own children. Every time we have sung it, it has conjured up a good feeling of conviviality and pleasure as I remembered the notes of that song emitting from the larynx of 100 youthful celebrants.

What then has this to do with the discovery of the ultimate purpose? All of us are complex combinations of our environment. With this little experience came a life-long feeling of being able to act silly and frivolous under relaxing situations. This is a great attribute when you have children. I don't mean acting ridiculous or immature. What I do mean is being able to enter into the fun and thrill of a game or activity at any level of any group. Without this ability, I would say it is quite difficult to have satisfying group relationships at any level of life.

In the years that ensued, I have observed literally hundreds of people who are afraid to be laughed at or afraid to laugh at themselves. They hang around on the edges of groups, desperately wanting to be a part of the group, but afraid to let their life and vitality show. Often their rationale is:

"I don't think they want me in the game."

"If they act like that, I don't want any part of it."

"Well, if he is going to cut me down all the time, I'll just leave and nobody will miss me."

"They don't like me anyway."

The sad part of the whole thing is, when one starts to develop a pattern of this kind of thinking and attitude, the above statements tend to be true. Little does the person realize the things he is saying are true because he is making them come true. All it would take is a positive attitude and some experience like I have mentioned in my youth for him to turn his entire social life completely around.

Let me summon one more anecdote, not for any particular purpose, but it is one which I rather enjoy drawing the word picture.

It always seems that when things go wrong, they really go wrong. Such a day happened in my freshmen year of school. My brother was pulling out of a parking space on Sheean Street, and John and I were in the back seat talking. In the front, my brother was driving, his girlfriend, center, and Jack Jones on shotgun. The car was a black (what else?) Chevy, floor shift (also, what else?) We roared out of the parking space and whipped onto Sheean, picking up speed as we approached Main. Faster, faster, John and I were beginning to feel uneasy as we came closer to the stop sign at the busy intersection. It was right after school, busses were zipping back and forth through the intersection, and students were eager to leave the area. Closer and faster we came. Finally, Jack asked in a rather shaky voice, "Aren't you going to stop?"

My brother answered as we missed a northbound bus by inches and a southbound squealed to a stop as we went over the curb between the light pole and the restraining wall of Jerry's Ice Cream Palace, "Sure would like to!"

My brother had installed clutch and brake extensions and his shoe strings were caught on the bolts on the underside of the brake and the clutch. He simply could not get his feet on top to activate the pedals.

The car went along the sidewalk on the south side of Jerry's and finally came to rest with the front fender smashed against the broken fireplug at Adams Street. Water, water everywhere! Coleridge would have loved it.

The only thing that sank, however, was John and I away from the scene of the crime.

The police were there taking names and addresses and all that kind of useless information. I told my brother to meet us over in the Sears parking lot behind the school. After several minutes, my brother came swinging into the parking lot. We hopped into the back seat, and my brother threw it into reverse and jammed down on the accelerator. John and I were thrown against the back window of the car as we crashed into one of the concrete supports of one of the massive parking lot lights. My brother had backed into this concrete buttress with the force of a Sherman tank.

I got out with the rest to check the damage to the auto. The left rear fender was shoved in quite badly. We decided all of us would go over to Jack's house and pound out the fender that night after dinner.

The evening grew later than we had planned. About 10:00pm, the "Black Beauty" traveling east on Washington Street stopped at the light at South Filmore. During the shifting time at that intersection, my brother tried to shift out of third. When he yanked on the lever, it came right out of the floor. Thus, the car was permanently in third gear. Starting from a dead stop in third gear is no easy task. To accomplish this, my brother did a lot of clutch burning and engine racing. It smelled! However, once in third, the ride is smooth and uneventful until one slowed or tried to slowly go up hills.

A picture of the terrain is here in order.

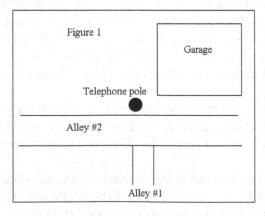
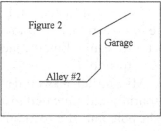

My brother wanted the car in the garage so we could pound out the dent. There was a slight incline about two feet from the garage. (see fig. 2). Those who have some knowledge of the principles of inertia now can visualize the problem. To come down alley #2 and make a sharp left up the incline in third gear was impossible. The only other option was to come in alley #1 at a higher rate of speed, make the jog, miss the telephone pole and go up the incline and into the garage.

He decided to attempt this last maneuver so down alley #1 the black bomb came. My brother ground the clutch to pick up speed. Traveling rather fast for a narrow alley, the telephone pole loomed imposingly ahead. With my brother at the wheel, the car was guided into the jog and bounced up the steep, short, incline. He hit the brakes hard, but too late and the inertia was too great. The car went halfway through the back wall. Two by fours, siding, insulation, and glass were strewn over the windshield.

Not to be daunted, we then began the process of pounding out of the fenders. But it was now almost midnight, and the noise started to blink on the lights in the neighborhood. A black and white car with red lights on top pulled silently towards us down alley #2.

THIS, I THINK, COULD BE CLASSIFIED AS A BAD DAY.

XXIV

God Pulls the String on the Net

Since there's no help, come let us kiss and part.
Nay, I have done; you get no more of me,
And I am glad, yea, glad with all my heart,
That thus so cleanly I myself can free.
Michael Drayton

What then of life's purpose? How has the ever tightening net been strung to include me? What direction should life take and which way should I go to life's ultimate triumph?

At this time, generally speaking, I was living pretty much the way I wanted to live. My Christian experience was a rather dismal failure. I was not living the victorious Christian life that should normally come when someone has connected with the Infinite. I spent my time in the pursuits of the pleasures of life and fun, more or less forgetting the Son of God in my life.

If someone were to ask me at that time if I was happy and having fun, I would, of course, have answered yes, very much so. I didn't care to go back to the arrangement that so characterized my early Christian walk after my conversion.

Perhaps the experience that so crystallized my inner thinking and finally led to the collapse of all my godly defenses happened while "necking" with a girl in a parked car on the east side of Belaire. How best to describe the salient parts of this affair in a delicate manner is difficult. At the outset, let me state that nothing of any terminal sexual nature occurred.

My 8th grade teacher whipped me because of an untruth concerning my relationship with this girl. Someone had told Mr. Nooze I was necking with the girl in one of the rooms at the school . . . his room. He really believed the incident occurred and whipped me for it. This incident alienated me from the girl's parents also. It was not so much that I wouldn't have done this or that she was not willing, but we lacked opportunity. (Take note parents). Anyway, the incident did not happen, and I was unjustly accused and punished, but such are many experiences as we "shuffle along this mortal coil."

As we traveled through high school, I always kept her available in case I ever needed a date or a car. Believe it or not, sometimes she would stop by and pick me up; then I would drop her off and use her car for the rest of the evening to pick up other girls. She never griped about this, and I suppose she thought she loved me. I did not love her and looking back, I suppose I let her hang around me for several reasons.

1. She was a beautiful girl and it was flattering to my ego to have her at my command.
2. I always had someone when I needed a date.
3. I used her to further my own ends and to gain socially and economically.

All of them wrong reasons I know, but analysis of the whole situation would be useless without being totally objective as to motives and operation.

Simple Algebra now follows: $a+b+c+d+e=$ an explosive sexual situation. Sufficed to say, I physically thought the idea was an appealing one.

The love of man and woman surely must have more to it than the mutual massaging of one another's reproductive organs for a short period. It should be a time of total giving not just physically, but emotionally, spiritually, mentally and psychologically. It is a time of facing the world completely as a unit, a time of one bolstering the weaknesses of the other with his own strengths, a time of communication and sharing of mutual interests. It is definitely a time of uniqueness, total oneness, if you may. We are meant to be a single unit for a lifetime, not just two people living their lives from one life crisis to another by means of bedroom climaxes.

This whole thinking process took about thirty seconds. The absurdity and futility of the whole affair then came into sharp focus.

I want to carefully note the whole process of rational thought not once took into consideration the wants, needs or future of the girl. I was absolutely selfish with my thoughts. This thought then smashed into my brain like a sledgehammer. If I had any thoughts that this was love, they were dashed to smithers by the thought of my own selfishness.

Here is a good test for love. Ask yourself the following question, "Is this act or thought grounded in giving me pleasure or profit, or is it for the good or joy of the person to whom the act or thought is directed?" If the answer is for my pleasure or profit, the relationship with the person involved is probably not a love relationship. Love keeps giving, today, tomorrow and forever. Giving and giving—giving emotionally, spiritually, financially, and last of all, physically.

Love involves a commitment of the will. It involves discipline, time, sharing, study and hard work. Not only a commitment of the body, but love includes all the emotions and ramifications of the material and spiritual spheres of our world.

Love is eternal, connected with the God-Head for God is love. The eternal truths of God are found in the experiences of true loving. God has described his relationship with man in the metaphors and terms of the human marriage relationship. No more excellent description of this relationship has been given since the Holy Spirit told us through the Apostle Paul that man ought to love his wife as Christ loves the church. Also, that a man who does not provide for his own family is worse than an infidel.

As I look back on the situation, it would seem somewhat of a blow to the ego to have offered yourself physically to someone and then have your offering completely rejected. I suppose not a whole lot unlike Cain as he came bringing an offering in his sin and selfishness. The offering, brought in the right context of God's laws and our obedience to Him, can be a pure and solidly spiritual as well as physical experience, but brought outside of God's laws, like Cain, will cause nothing but further degeneration of our physical and eternal state.

Why should this be included? In my judgment, I believe it was the final scene in the drama which was being written, staged and directed by the Almighty. He was now ready to ring down the curtain on any objections that might be still lingering in my mind about His taking over of my life.

I had known the thrill of physical activity, athletics, the thrill of cruelty, the joy of a happy home, the thrill of solid work, the security of money and wealth, the conviviality of friends and social life, the pleasure of a sexual experience, even though defaulted, and the pleasure of intelligence and education. Every one of these things left me cold and spiritually lifeless. As I have just penned these last words, my mind reverts to Ecclesiastes and the words of Solomon. Just now as I reread those words, it seems that the previous paragraph could have been the rewording of Ecclesiastes 1:17-3:6. How often we read something in the Scripture and are guilty of saying God surely does not know anything about which He is talking. Then as life proceeds, we tend to come full circle to the same conclusion God has reached an eternity ago. What time and heartache we could salvage if we just took Him at his word.

God had now broken the last cord that had held me to the traditional position of youthful lusts and thinking. I now knew there was nothing left to keep God out. The inevitable had come, the day I had feared. The day of final reckoning with the infinite God concerning this life He had given me was at the gate of my being. I knew I was doomed. I didn't know how it would happen, but I did know that it would happen. When, how, where, who or what would be the instrument, I didn't know. I was resigned, dejected and depressed. I felt like my life was over. I was confused and horribly ill-prepared to face school, home, or work.

My life started to fall apart as news of the park experience began to leak out to our group. I had hoped that it could be quietly forgotten; it wasn't. I had hoped to escape the derision of my group for not taking the golden opportunity for which every young buck has dreamed.

My schoolwork fell off, and I felt trapped in a cage not of my own making.

WHY . . . WHAT . . . WHEN?

XXV

The Lightning Strikes

If you have tears, prepare to shed them now.
Shakespeare

The matter I am about to recount sounds so simple, but is yet so complex, so very complex. It was a matter of such short duration but has changed the direction of my entire life.

As I have said, God, for some long period had been bringing the net of His being ever closer to my struggling existence. I, like a fish, had been swimming along searching for food for the soul, turning this way and that into various pleasurable experiences. At every turn of the brook, at every choice morsel eaten, I found the haunting strains of the voice of God saying, "This is not it, move on".

And so on and on I moved, each experience savored, checked off and discarded. Shortly after the experience of the previous chapter, it happened, so smoothly, so naturally yet like a bolt of lightning from out of a cloudless sky.

I remember that night as if it were yesterday. So clear is this thought that I even think I could remember the color of the furnishings in the room and the pictures on the wall. I have been over this experience so much in my mind that the event is engraved somewhere in those electro circuits for all eternity.

February 1956, the last night of the sectional, Chick and I had gone to the game.

For anyone not living in Indiana, a definition of sectional is in order. The sectional is the first stepping stone for a basketball team on its way to the state championship. That statement does not in anyway do justice to the idea of the sectional! Late February and March in Indiana is sometimes called "Hoosier Hysteria." It is a time for students, teachers and adults to go absolutely mad. I have seen small towns build 7000 to 8000 seat gymnasiums just to have the privilege of hosting a sectional or stealing it from a neighboring town with a smaller gym.

I have seen riots in gyms, stoning of officials, friends from different school districts not talking to one another, and stealing of players by bribes of job offers to their parents. I have known of incidents of cars bearing the license plates of the winning town being literally shredded by losing fans. I have never heard of murder being committed, but I do know of beatings and group rumbles of fans as they left the melee.

Sometimes when a team won the sectional, the school was usually closed for a while if not all day on the Monday thereafter. Almost always this was the case for a regional win and a necessity for a Semi-state and State Championship.

We had a good team in '56. We had previously won the city championship. Our school was, for a period of about six years in the mid-fifties, a state powerhouse in basketball.

Back to the fateful evening. Chick and I left early for the arena to get the choice spots for the game. We were playing John Adams High School, the archrival of all that is good or decent in this world and the personification of evil and badness. (Now there is rivalry).

The sectional championship game was at 8:15 but we arrived about 6:30 to claim good seats and to hustle a date for the party after the game. The game was a hot one and the lead seesawed a record number of times. Finally, the horn sounded and Jefferson beat the hated villains. The stands emptied out onto the floor. Everyone assaulted the nets with scissors and knives. The winning crowd was completely out of control as they flooded the hallways toward the locker rooms. The half hour wait seemed short as the team came out quickly to greet their subjects. They were mobbed completely, but loved every minute of it. It was a frenzied moment of ecstasy as most emotions were out of control.

Chick and I had two girls (whose names have long left me) with us as we headed to the after party. The brown Merc pulled into the long driveway that led up to a small estate. Leafless maple trees line the entrance road for almost 1000 feet. The moon was high and not quite full.

As the car stopped, we could hear the music blasting out the popular song, "It's Almost Tomorrow."

It's almost tomorrow,
but what can I do,
your kisses all tell me
your love is untrue.

I'll love you forever
till stars cease to shine
and hope someday darling,
that your love will be mine.

I still find myself singing that song when I lapse into fits of nostalgia. Little did I know that it was almost tomorrow for me, but it had nothing to do with kisses or girls or that kind of falderal.

I exited the car with the others to enter the party. A song titled "Because of You" was now on the HI-FI with full amplification.

I remember every detail, every thought, every word, every eye picture, every noise, local geography, furnishings, and colors of the next scene.

Chick and the girls had gone ahead a few yards, and I was just sauntering along aimlessly. I walked toward the front entrance of the brown and cream Tudor house, a double dark green door indented 3 feet with a brass handle and door knocker in the center of both doors. There were three concrete steps to a slight landing and one step up to the door.

The dark green door opened into a foyer about twelve feet long and six feet wide. There was a dark walnut stained hall tree immediately to the left. Next, a den-like room with several easy chairs and a large desk was to one side. Continuing, there was a large open circular stairway to the upper two levels, a large mirror with a dark walnut stained table under the mirror. On both sides of the mirror were two large gold sconces. To my right was a large library table covered by a white lace cloth, and on the cloth were two candlesticks with dark green candles. A little farther to my right was a large opening arch into a big living room. The room dropped one step from the arch onto a landing and then down three steps into a lush living, room. The carpet was a dark green print and theme of lighter greens and lighter colors was evident in drapes, chairs and sofas.

I stood in the arch at the top step and looked out into the room. The beer was already flowing and the liquor cabinet lock had been broken. Stretched out over chairs and sofa were boys and girls in various states of inebriation and undress. I didn't see the HI-FI, but I could certainly hear it. The loud booming voice of Elvis was bellowing forth from somewhere in the bowels of this gigantic house.

The cigarette and cigar smoke had obliterated the room with a low-hanging blue fog, and Chick and the girls had disappeared somewhere inside. I looked out into the fog and something hit me like a lightning bolt. The Holy Spirit convicted me like a ton of bricks falling on my head. The guilt was overwhelming, the fear of God's punishment was more than I could bear.

I mumbled aloud, "My God, what in the Hell am I doing here?"

I whirled on my heels and walked back out into the cool air to clear my head. I leaned against the trellis to the left of the concrete walk, whispering the following prayer. "Oh God, somewhere, wherever you are, hear me. Draw close to my being because I need you so. I've made such a mess out of the life that You've given to me. Now if there is anything you can do with this life, anything you can salvage from the wreck I've made, then it's yours, use it; I'm done. I've had it."

I walked out to Chick's car and took off. After driving for about twenty minutes, I went home. I parked Chick's car in my driveway and walked up to my room. I sat at the window of my room until nearly 4am. Sometime around 1am, someone started Chick's car and drove it away. I watched the moon and thought for hours.

Unlike the first experience I had with God back in 1949, the change this time was radical, quick and long lasting. However, like the previous experience, there was very little emotion or high feeling. The only emotion or bolt was the conviction and guilt I felt at the top of the stairs several hours earlier.

Now, there was no guilt, no depression, only the feeling that calmness and serenity had finally caught up with me. I was at ease. God had finally caught me in the love of His Son, Jesus Christ. Or better, I had finally given accent and put my trust in the living resurrected Christ for my salvation and eternal destiny. I had finally made connection with the Infinite. My life now had a new dimension, a new direction. Yes, it was new life both now and eternally.

The change of thought process was immediate, but the new life certainly did not solve my problems. In fact, it did nothing noticeably for them at all. All it did was show me the mental, physical, and spiritual attitude I should have toward those problems. Some might infer by this statement that I don't believe in God's miraculous intervention in our lives here. Nothing could be farther from the truth. Actually, the changing of my attitudes, desires, direction and purpose was in itself a miracle of rank one! I have seen God's touch in my life and in others in a supernatural way.

In my judgment, one of the greatest tragedies and fallacies of the evangelical church today is the presentation of Christianity as the panacea to all of life's problems and the situations in which one is floundering. Some say, if you give to God, He will give to you materially. If you need healing, He will heal you. If you are persecuted, He will annihilate the persecutor. If you have robbed a bank and killed a guard, He will get you off scott-free and square you with the law. This kind of thinking is misleading to the Christian and absurdity to the unbeliever. The Christian life is not a cure for all of life's headaches, persecutions and tribulation. If it is, I fear when the first tribulation comes, those cure-all people will drop by the wayside in despair and disgust at the thought of God having ever proposed a solution for their life.

In my own case, I came to God expecting nothing. I came in complete knowledge that I could do nothing more with myself. I came knowing that He would do what was best for my life. I came in fear because I saw what He is, compared to what I am. I came in love realizing what He had already done for me. I came, in willingness, knowing what the Christian life meant in terms of purity and holiness. I came knowing the old gnawings of depression, fear, and distrust would probably at times still haunt me. At these times, though, if God was who He said He was, He would meet these thoughts head on with truth like, "Do not despair my son, I have the situation well in hand and you are only a pilgrim passing through this land. You search for a city and I am the builder and maker of that city. I have promised that whatever comes to you is ordered by me, and nothing will come to you that you cannot bear. Even this will be for your good in the end. I've clothed the flowers and the birds, and they don't even work. Why then do you think that I can't take care of you? I'll be with you forever, I'll never forsake you. I'll be with you even when you walk through that starry shadow called physical death. You're mine, nobody can take you away from me. My Spirit has witnessed with your spirit that we are one just like Jesus, my own beloved Son and I are one. You are an inheritor of everything I have because you have trusted your life in His hands. When I look at you and your failings and imperfections, I look at them through the eternal sacrifice of My Son's own blood. When I do this, I see you in His perfection and His Holiness and Purity. Thus, in My sight, you are completely made clean and His perfection is put on your account."

Now when these thoughts come, it is the time for emotion, joy unspeakable, and full of GLORY, the song of the soul set free. I think this is the same feeling of joy and shouting that my father had so many years earlier in that cornfield. I see now the emotion had nothing to do with impressing God or getting His attention, but rather, as my father had said, "The realization of your own soul redeemed is completely overwhelming."

I cannot bear that feeling without some emotion for it is tremendous and eternal, joy unspeakable and full of glory.

XXVI

Beginnings, Again

Being full of assurance that what He had promised,
He was able to perform.
Saint Paul

What now of the purpose of life, the joy of living? I found that cold night in February only a start of the direction I should be going. I might say it was just a realization of the path that leads to glory. I'm still on that road; the way is still hard and difficult, but now I have Someone who has walked that road before me and now walks along with me. He tells me where the pitfalls and rough spots are. He says turn left or right or watch for road signs. We talk together and have good times. I listen and He speaks, mostly through His Word (the Scriptures). Also, He speaks through His servants, scholars and other Christians, through His servants' works, Christian books that are in harmony with Scripture, through my thoughts, reason and experiences, (though these are least reliable). Finally, He speaks by my spiritual meditation. It is this time of meditation which has been most sweet and pure.

So God is still chipping away at my life even now as I pen this work some twenty-five years later. The thrill or joy and purpose He gave me is still there. The haunting yearning that so plagued by soul in the early years in gone. In its place, God has given me a Holy dissatisfaction with my life and surroundings. This feeling, not at all like the youthful one of despair, tends to express itself in the idea that God has a grand design for my existence. Whether it is to preach to millions, to be a great philanthropist endowing thousands of mission boards, scholarly study of His word, or just day-in-and-day-out living His life in mine and conveying it to my children and friends, I don't know. But what I do know is that He has called me to this High Calling in Christ Jesus and I want to be worthy of our mutual choice of each other.

> Am I a soldier of the cross,
> A follower of the lamb?
> And shall I fear to own His cause,
> Or blush to speak His name?
>
> Must I be carried to the skies
> on flowery beds of ease
> While others fought to win the prize,
> And sailed through bloody seas?
>
> Are there no foes for me to face?
> Must I not stem the flood?
> Is this vile world a friend to Grace,
> To help me on to God?
>
> Sure I must fight, If I would reign;
> Increase my courage, Lord:
> I'll bear the toil, endure the pain,
> Supported by Thy Word."
> Isaac Watts

XXVII

Epilogue

What though the radiance which was once so bright
Be now forever taken from my sight,
Though nothing can bring back the hour
Of splendor in the grass, of glory in the flower;
We will grieve not, rather find
Strength in what remains behind;
William Wordsworth

The final days of my senior year were extremely happy ones. For a time during 1956-57, I spent hours at the church talking with my Pastor and the church office help. I suppose they got tired of me showing up about two times a week, but I think here is where both church and school are lacking.

Our church had a very lackluster program that was not meeting the needs of the group. Men like Harvey Higgins, who had the desire to get to know and love the kids at their level, did the real youth work. Perhaps the toughest pill for me to swallow personally is to accept kids at the point at which we meet and work with them from there.

The church program was to put each kid in the straight jacket of the system without God changing his attitudes, aims, goals, desires and life. In reality, this, I believe is the reverse of Christ's work with people while he was on earth.

The youth program, I believe, should be geared to individual identification with a non-adolescent for each child. This non-adolescent must be solidly Christian without blemish to society. Children quickly realize if the person is no better than he is, why then should he listen to him. For boys, this person must be manly and active. High school boys need movement, action and sometimes, even roughness. For the girls, this person must be feminine and active.

At this point, an aside concerning the national insanity of women's liberation might be in order. The idea that women and men are physically comparable is biologically absurd, mentally deprecating, and scripturally heretical. Functionally, the roles of men and women, even though of equal importance, are as different as their physical and psychological make-up. The idea that man is the head of the house and the woman is in obeisance or is second in command is as old as God himself. To even argue the point is to argue with God, for He clearly teaches this method of family authority.

As the three months toward graduation began to slip away, I began to see a very important thing happening in my social life. The full social life I had before the events of the sectional night, I still desired to have. I still wanted to be friends with my group and go out to Roco's and the like, but I noticed a curious thing about the Christian life. I found that though I didn't say a word, the guys began to see the change in my life was not a flash-in-the-pan. So as they began to think of their nefarious activities (that were sometimes illegal and often immoral), they included me less and less.

Here is an important point. In the years that have passed, I have always been suspect about people claiming loudly that they are Christian, bold and wonderful, and having friends that are definitely not. Christ said, "We are in the world not of it. What has light to do with darkness or God with Mammon." I thoroughly believe that as a Christian, I am to go where sinners are and to be personable, loving and friendly; however, day in and day out communication of a friendly basis is impossible between Christian and non-Christian. This, I think, constitutes approval with their activities, pleasures, and desires.

Quite obviously then, the professing Christian who has a large number of social contacts on a personal individual basis with non-Christians either:

1. Does not understand the Christian life and is not living the way God has commanded in His word, or
2. Is not a Christian at all and is just fooling himself and those about him.

Because of this truth, during the last month of high school I found myself outside of the mainstream of social life. I started turning more and more to the group that I knew to be Christian, although their acceptance of me was a little like the Christians accepting Paul after his conversion. For me, though, Ttese social contacts were relatively inconsequential because:

1. I thought these kids were weird and
2. I knew in six months I would be in college where I could concentrate on making friendships that would last a lifetime.

I define many of the Christians in high school as different mainly because it is my contention God has not called every high school Christian to be an evangelist. For the church or parents to think that their young Christian prodigy is going to preach and win the whole high school is wishful thinking. True, youngsters should give a solid Christian testimony and stand up for God and His righteousness, but to lead the whole school to Christ is, I think, rather ill advised.

First, the child has none of the Christian maturity it takes to stand the ridicule and remain normal. Second, the child does not have the experience to deal with the many different kinds of personal problems he will encounter in an in depth reaching of the high school student. Third, the child does not have the knowledge of Scripture or depth of mature interpretation that leads a person along the heavenly path. Let me be quick to state that I am sure kids leading other kids to Christ does and should happen, but not, I believe, in the large-scale way a mature Christian of outgoing temperament can do later in life.

One can clearly establish this point by example in both the Old and New Testaments. Before he was brought forth as God's man for the hour, God prepared Moses for eighty years. David spent long years of trial and travail between the time Samuel anointed him as God's chosen king and the time he actually came to the throne. Samuel himself spent long years of preparation from the time he was chosen of God one lonely night in his bed as a child and the time he became the chosen beloved leader and prophet of Israel. New Testament examples include Paul's years in the wilderness, the apostles' time with Christ from their choosing until Pentecost, and especially Peter as he went from mush-mouthed trickster to God's appointed man. All took time to walk and talk with God and saturate themselves with the Word of God. Only then were they presented to the public, ready to lead, interpret and guide sinners to repentance along the tangled path to glory.

The Christian life takes time, study, patience, hard work, and discipline, like any other endeavor that is worthwhile in our lives. It was this patience that I was learning as began to associate with those of like faith during these few short weeks from April until college.

Here is one amusing anecdote from this period. The church had a senior banquet which was to be an all night affair. I, like the others, had made a date for the evening with a raven-tressed beauty in whom I had been interested for a short time. I think she and her parents had been interested in me for some time because the moment I asked her out, the rumor mill had us at the altar, repeating nuptial vows. Her parents kept having me over for dinner and asking my parents out as well. My policy had always been to be very careful when a girl's parents became interested in me. I always felt that one of two things was happening and both of them were bad.

1. The parents suspected I was playing hanky-panky and they were placing me in such a position that should anything "turn up" they were prepared to swallow me up in suffocating niceness. This supposedly would keep me from hurting the daughter or skipping out on the situation.
2. The parents thought that I was a desirable bridegroom for their daughter. Since the poor girl had very few other chances, (or had some and let them get away), the parents were to make sure that I was not going to escape the bliss of a lifetime with their sweet darling daughter.

It was the second kind of situation in which I found myself the evening of the Senior Banquet at our church.

The evening was well planned. The banquet was from at 8:00pm until 10:00pm when everyone was to change clothes and meet back at the church at 11:00pm for a scavenger hunt. After the instructions, the hunt would begin at midnight. Then the group was to meet at Carl Friskem's home at 4:00am for ping-pong, pool, food and games. At 5:30am, we were to return to the church for breakfast. By 8:00am, the party was over and everyone was free to go about their own activities.

The scavenger hunt was the only flaw in the whole plan. Everyone received a copy of the starting point of the hunt. This was to lead us through a series of places all over the city of Belaire to pick up a note at each place. The first one to the Friskem's home was the winner. Our group was doing quite well until we hit the third note.

About 3:00am, I wheeled into the cemetery on Marshall Road as the rest of the cars turned in behind me. Each one of us started looking around for a certain name on a tombstone. I moved around from stone to stone for about fifteen minutes until one of our group yelled that he had found it about eighty yards to the right of where I was.

At about that moment, I looked up and pulling into the cemetery were two sherriff's cars and a state trooper. Red lights, spot lights and head lights were flashing everywhere!

It seems that some neighbors had seen the lights in the cemetery and had called the police. Also, it seems that in the State of Indiana, there is a law prohibiting the entrance to grave yards from sundown to sunrise.

The officers then asked the entire group to drive to the Friskem home, the place where we were to terminate the game. All of us, including the Assistant Pastor, were questioned and our names, addresses and parents' names were taken and recorded. We had pretty glum looks on our faces as we ate and played pool and ping-gong.

The officers told us the sexton would check the cemetery for damage as soon as dawn arrived. If there was any damage, whether we had done it or not, we would he responsible.

The next evening, I was sitting on my front porch waiting for my father to come home from work. He arrived and I began the long, tenuous process of telling of the past night's activities. After I had confessed my part in being in the cemetery after dark, he stopped me and said, "I know, the Pastor and I already talked today. Now don't worry about it since you did no damage or were not planning on being malicious." That was the end of it between my father and me on this incident, but I suspect that the church council discussed it at some length.

Two items appear to me out of this rather benign incident. First, I learned something about parents that helped me and I believe, also made me a better parent. On the whole, parents are not really as ignorant of their offspring's activities as youngsters would tend to think. How could they be????? The network and facilities parents have at their command for checking on their young people is awesome. It has always amazed me as a parent the vast amounts of information I can pick up about my children with such little effort. True, most of this information is post-facto and as such is anti-climatic, and thus, can only be used in two ways.

1. Information purely for information sake to file away for future reference of behavior patterns.
2. To be used as a lever, to show your offspring that "I really know what's going on." Hopefully, this lever will make him think the next time he is trying any dastardly deed that Dad and Mom might know what I am doing just now. Even more powerful than this, though, is the truth that God is an ever-present being knowing all the child does, And what he thinks also.

Second, my father knew the problem before he acted. So many parents and adults act on impulse before the facts are all in. My father knew the situation pretty thoroughly having talked to both our Senior Pastor and the police, yet he let me tell him what I thought had happened.

This, I fear, is the crisis point at which the schism of the generation gap occurs. Children may be as wrong as sin, needing discipline, punishment, a good spanking, grounding or whatever discipline necessary for the individual child; but more than this, he needs to tell to his parents the facts of the case as he saw them. The child's interpretation of these facts is, more times than not, rationally inadequate. The parent then needs to point out the poor rationale and immaturity in a calm logical way. This alone is not enough. Discipline must follow in a loving way, if discipline is necessary.

In my judgment, these daily one-to-one encounters teach values and truth. The child needs and wants boundaries set by an authority figure. In my experience, without these boundaries, the child has difficulty adapting to the rules of society and the harsh reality of physical and spiritual laws over which he has no control.

XXVIII

The End of an Era

The moving finger writes;
And having writ, moves on.
The Rubaiyat of Omar Khayyam

Ivy Day, the awards day came though I wanted desperately to hold it back. Mr. B set a new World's Record with his typing awards. The ivy was planted without incident. The last big hurdle was the senior interview, then the senior banquet and graduation.

The senior interview was of enormous importance. At this time, I was to meet the mystery man of the school, the principal. If we were to meet on the street, we recognized one another but that was all. At school, I only saw the principal once before, in an official capacity as he gave six of us the boot for three days for a rather minor infraction of the truancy rules. I always knew if I met him in an official capacity, three or more days of forced vacation was the result. My day for the senior interview came. The office gave me a pass out of Latin, an event in itself unheard of during my time at Jefferson.

The senior interview consisted of three major parts. First, Principal Jones spoke of the traditions of Jefferson High School and the pride of her graduates. He then cautioned concerning the pitfalls of college and virtues of study and respectable behavior. His main concern was the fact which he emphasized most, the necessity for me to attend a school of higher education.

Most of the material in his first section, I already knew or had decided or really didn't care particularly. Not so with parts two and three. During this part of the discussion, we finally learned the hallowed scores of IQ, class rank, Kuder scale, Iowa scale, California Achievement, and all of the personal data that the school had in my file. I could read everything at will and pour over it for as long as I desired.

The third part of the discussion concerned the years that I had spent at Jefferson. Jones asked what areas I liked best and those I found disgusting and arbitrary. A funny thing happened to me when ask the second part of that question. As I sat there, I couldn't think of a single thing that was disgusting or I detested about the school. I am sure there were things that bugged me at the time, but for an answer to that question, I could not think of one thing about which I would like to gripe. My mental attitude really had changed and I found myself so wishing that the future would never come for I enjoyed the present so greatly.

But it came. Baccalaureate and Elgar's classic symbol of termination bid the days of adolescence goodbye . . .

FOREVER . . .

XXIX

Finale

Two roads diverged in a yellow wood,
And sorry I could not travel both
And be one traveler, long I stood
And looked down one as far as I could
To where it bent in the undergrowth;

Then took the other, as just as fair,
And having perhaps the better claim,
Because it was grassy and wanted wear;
Though as for that the passing there
Had worn them really about the same,

And both that morning equally lay
In leaves no step had trodden black.
Oh, I kept the first for another day!
Yet knowing how way leads on to way,
I doubted if I should ever come back.

I shall be telling this with a sigh
Somewhere ages and ages hence:
Two roads diverged in a wood, and I—
I took the one less traveled by,
<u>And that has made all the difference.</u>

Robert Frost

God had drawn me by some mysterious force into His Grand Design to Himself. It seems strange even to think that in all of His power and majesty and infinite knowing, He would care about my hopes, my likes, dislikes, or even my personal health, and wealth, let alone my eternal well-being. In my search for the ultimate thrill, joy and purpose in life, I found this God to not only be just and strict in His interpretation of Himself and world in which I live, but also a loving, personal, feeling entity who in Himself satisfied His own requirements for my salvation using a separate manifestation of His own Being whom I know as Jesus Christ, the Son of God.

This treatise has been concerned primarily with this search and the direction my life took because of it. The basic ideas were those of my life, but in some instances amplified to create continuity and reader interest.

The results are still being produced by the climatic end to my search on that cold night in February 1956. I have only taken the reader through the adolescent years. From high school graduation on contains the picture of the daily walk with Christ that has been so sweet, lo, these many years. It is this Christian walk that I propose to discuss in a later work. Deo Volente.

Sweetser, Indiana
April 5, 1976
RSO